Rebuilding Public Confidence
in Educational Assessment

Rebuilding Public Confidence in Educational Assessment

Mary Richardson

First published in 2022 by
UCL Press
University College London
Gower Street
London WC1E 6BT

Available to download free: www.uclpress.co.uk

ISBN: 978-1-78735-726-6 (Hbk.)
ISBN: 978-1-78735-725-9 (Pbk.)
ISBN: 978-1-78735-724-2 (PDF)
ISBN: 978-1-78735-727-3 (epub)
ISBN: 978-1-78735-728-0 (mobi)
DOI: https://doi.org/10.14324/111.9781787357242

For Adam, for everything

Contents

List of figures and tables

Figures

Table

Acknowledgements

My thanks go to the Philosophy of Education Society of Great Britain for the writing retreat in 2019 where this all got going; such time and space to think was invaluable.

Thanks to all of my family, but particularly my siblings, Dominic, Liz, Pat and Matthew – I know you still see me as the 'baby' of the tribe, but it's a badge I wear with pride and you have all given me brilliant examples of how to be and think in different ways (#highachieving-youngestchild). Thanks to Mum, for quiet and constant encouragement, coupled with such immense intelligence, and to Dad (1931–2020), because I know you are looking on with quiet pride and saying 'Read, Mouse, read – it's all there in books'.

Adam, thank you for being you, but especially for homemade bread when it's needed.

Thanks to the three best friends a girl could have: Helen and Emma (who made cocktails, emailed, called and listened to me moan), and t'other Mary (who said 'Get on with it' at the right times). The 'band' (Neil, Oli and Lewis) has a special place. Your collective belief in me has been sustaining – we can start 'gigging' again soon.

Colleagues at UCL Institute of Education, thank you: Ruth Dann, Tina Isaacs, Catarina Correia, Arthur Chapman, Amos Paran, Cosette Crisan, Jennie Golding, Jane Perryman, Kim Insley, Nicky Platt – you all encouraged me, often without realising. In the assessment 'world', special thanks go to Grace Grima, Rose Clesham and Martin Johnson for inspiration, and to Tom Anderson for his useful conversations about the nature of trust.

A very special, enormous thank you to Iain Marshall, for incisive reading and questioning, and to Mary Healy, whose sharp philosophical mind brought many ideas out of the long grass and into the light during drafting.

Thanks to Fourbears Books in Caversham – a wonderful independent bookshop with a brilliant reading space for children – and thanks to the many respondents on the children's literature forums who sent me lists of suggested reading about schools and testing in popular fiction.

Thanks to the education journalists and social media commentators who gave their time to talk to me about their views on assessment.

Final thanks go to Pat Gordon-Smith. You are an endlessly wise, cheerful and hilarious editor – any mistakes in this book are mine alone, because you and your team have done nothing but be amazing.

List of abbreviations

AfL   Assessment for Learning
HESA   Higher Education Statistics Agency
ILSA   International Large-Scale Assessments
NAPLAN   National Assessment Program – Literacy and Numeracy
             (in Australia)
OECD   Organisation for Economic Co-operation and Development
Ofqual   Office of Qualifications and Examinations Regulation
             (in England)
PIRLS   Progress in International Reading Literacy Study
PISA   Programme for International Student Assessment
SAT   Standard Attainment Test
TIMSS   Trends in International Mathematics and Science Study

Glossary

Throughout this book, the following definitions are used:

educational assessment	an overarching term to describe gathering evidence and reviewing this in line with criteria, in order to make a judgement or a decision about student learning; it includes all methods of assessment – from examinations to classroom tests, observations and so on
formative assessment	any assessment that collects data which can be used to support and direct learning, most commonly from teachers in a classroom setting at any level
high-stakes testing	summative tests that relate to certification and selection; their results will influence the choices and opportunities for the taker of the test
summative assessment	any assessment taken at the end of a course of study that generally results in a grade, most commonly in the form of examinations or tests

Introduction to confidence issues in educational assessment

In June 2013, I was conducting research in Finland. It was part of a longitudinal study with six European partner universities, and we had spent a week together writing and planning. On the final day, the weather was uncharacteristically hot for the Arctic Circle and, given the option of an indoor university tour or a trip to Santa's village, we all chose the latter.

The village includes shops and, of course, Santa's Post Office, where, after posting some cards, I wandered into the post room. I struck up a conversation with an 'elf' about the types of request they get and she showed me the files of letters, pulling out that year's collection from England. One letter, handwritten on pink notepaper (in typically girlish writing – very rounded, with hearts instead of dots above the letter 'i'), caught my eye. It said:

> *Dear Santa,*
> *What I'd like for Christmas is to get 10 A stars in my GCSEs. If I fail, I will*
> *let everyone down – they think I can do it. I try really hard at school but*
> *don't always get the grades I want. Please help Santa. Love, xxx*

I was struck by the fact that a child of 15 or 16 years old (the age when GCSE examinations are sat in England) was writing to a mythical figure for help and by the innate desperation of the request. This letter suggests that the pressure is too much, the expected level of achievement is wrong, and its presence is causing such anxiety that it led to this desperate cry for help.

Throughout this book, I use many examples from my own context in England, but I also include examples from international contexts, to demonstrate that we are facing a global crisis in education. The examples and focus for the issues in educational assessment are based on 'discourses' – the many ways in which we communicate and share ideas, and how we understand and make sense of the world. The letter to Santa not only reflects a discourse of high expectations (a desire to achieve top grades), it also reveals an opposing discourse framed by doom, of concern about letting people down or not being good enough.

It is important to understand that discourses are not the 'truth'; rather, they are narratives constructed by individuals or groups to try to characterise what is meant in a particular situation. What makes discourses problematic is when they become an accepted norm or an ideal that skews how people see and understand the world around them. In educational settings, this is definitely an issue. The theory of discourses in education is explained further in Chapter 1.

Globally, the emphasis on comparative achievement in educational assessment has become more prominent since the 1990s (Unterhalter, 2019). This has radically changed our perceptions about the aims and purpose of education, and has consequently impacted on how we view educational assessment. Essentially, assessment is characterised by a received culture of competition, leading to a belief that the grade is everything. This idea is so important now that some tests are called 'high-stakes' tests, because their results shape us: they determine our careers, our access to higher education, our access to certain opportunities and places, and our socio-economic prospects (Torrance, 2017). The addiction to high-stakes testing is often framed by claims (which lack substantive evidence) that exams are fairer and more rigorous than any other type of assessment, so they present a more truthful, measured picture of academic achievement of which we can be more confident.

Assessment and its outcomes matter deeply to us, so I am concerned by a global lack of confidence in both policy and practice. This low confidence comes from poor understanding of two things: what assessment is and how assessment works. These two deficits have preoccupied me for some time, and this book is an attempt to present some answers to each of them in an accessible, evidence-based way.

When I tell people that my work is in educational assessment, their response is either a barely disguised yawn or, more commonly, a barrage of questions about why national testing and standards have collapsed. Despite the notion that assessment is not a very interesting topic, it appears to preoccupy a great deal of public interest. It is time for an honest, clear explanation and conversation about its key constituents, while also challenging some of the misconceptions that emerge in public settings. Testing, particularly the examination system, is often in the news.

This leads me to question how something so influential can be regarded with suspicion and framed by challenges and anxiety.

Views of assessment are broadly influenced by a complex series of discourses that surround our understanding of its development, use and outcomes. However, an examination of popular discourses within public domains reveals an unsatisfying binary level of argument – a love–hate relationship with the whole idea of assessment. We 'love' the certification and selection that the results of standardised testing bring, but we 'hate' the extent to which grading and measuring from the same tests has the capacity to influence opportunities and can lead to personal labelling.

Much of the vast range of assessment literature that has evolved since the 1990s comprises evidence of how formative assessment could challenge our reliance on testing as 'the best' form of assessment and demonstrates that assessment can be a way of informing and supporting learning. But despite a plethora of resources and global engagement with the idea of assessment for learning theories, when the chips are down we do not necessarily engage with formative assessments; we prefer to rely on grades to summarise ability, skills or knowledge. Such patterns of behaviour are not unique to England, but are seen from Canada to Kazakhstan, and from Slovenia to Hong Kong. Grades are a universally accepted way of characterising achievement and understanding success in academic terms.

Much research has been conducted on this theme and it reveals consistent patterns of anxiety and pressure. Obsession with exams and the continual promotion of competition as a foundation for a sense of educational achievement has been noted as problematic since the 1950s (Fielding, 2011). Yet we continue to repeat the cycle. In England, Reay and Wiliam (1999) found that national testing schemes in English state-maintained primary schools were leading children to judge themselves based on their scores. Children were literally describing themselves as a 'four', or even a 'nothing'. Their scores referred to what was called the common attainment scale across the three key stages in education. These were numbered from 1 to 8, and the children in this study (aged about 10) were working towards a national average grade of 4, so anything below this would be considered a 'failure'. The study suggested a need to change the concern and to focus on test outcomes as a measure of potential.

However, this unhealthy obsession with grading at a young age continues. It is implicit in the public messaging shown in Figure 0.1, which appeared on an advertising hoarding at the end of my road.

Figure 0.1 *The Little Blue Book of Sunshine*. Source: Photograph by author, reproduced with kind permission of NHS Berkshire West (2020)

Clearly aimed at the teenagers who walk by it each day en route to the nearby secondary school, this advertisement promotes an online resource designed to provide support for anxious students. What surprised me about this is the order of concerns listed: exams are at the top of the list, outranking relationships – very different to my experience of teenage years at school!

There is an inconsistency in the perceived purpose of assessment clashing with a flawed understanding of a framework of educational achievement. Politicians and policymakers claim that our education system is now more sensitive than ever to the needs of all children, yet we accept a system of testing that is increasingly reductive. Those who create and produce our high-stakes examinations claim that such assessments provide balanced ways of capturing how students demonstrate knowledge, skills and/or understanding in the subjects they study in school. In terms of test construction, reliability and validity, this may be so, but how these tests demonstrate the achievements of individuals is more ethically troubling. Teachers are increasingly forced to focus their students' attention on grades and not necessarily because they matter to the student. Chapters 1 and 2 explain this issue and introduce the continual quest for an elusive gold standard.

This book is not an attempt to identify and challenge all of the ways in which we talk about educational assessment. Instead, I explore them using what I have identified as dominant discourses on screen, in print and online. There are literally hundreds of thousands of articles that analyse assessment in a range of ways – from the social and political, through policymaking, to technical construction and classroom practice. However, I am interested in how assessment is discussed broadly too. Look beyond the limited readerships of academic publishing and there are so many public discourses about this issue. There is no single, correct interpretation of those beliefs and perceptions that circulate how we talk about assessment, and I'm not seeking to reveal the right way that it should be undertaken. Rather, I want to try to understand the prevailing discourses, so that there are other ways to reflect on what is happening in this controversial and contested area of education.

Dual thinking about education

There is a binary theme running through this book: the idea of two ways to assess (summative and formative) and two ways to think of achievement (pass or fail). Essentially, this is a simplistic evaluation of how education and its outcomes are conceptualised and discussed. In public settings, discussions about assessment are often framed in a simple binary choice: for example, which is better, an exam or a teacher assessment? Or which is fairer, a standardised test or a performance piece? It is fine to pose such questions, but when we're trying to ascertain how confident we feel about assessment, they shouldn't be the only questions we ask.

One of the many things that make me curious about confidence in assessment is the type of information that now accompanies its use in schools. People often ask me about examination results. They will say things like: 'Standards have fallen, haven't they?' or 'You've got to admit that more people get into university with lower grades' or 'It's easy to challenge a grade and get it changed'. In reality, it appears that the more publicity is given to our qualifications systems and the awarding process, the more people struggle to ascertain the truth. This leads them to lack confidence in their structure and practice.

One constant in education is change. This is an obvious statement maybe, but perhaps not widely acknowledged, because it has become the

Table 0.1 Examples of binary views on assessment theory and practice.
Source: Author

Summative assessment	Formative assessment
• Summative assessments, e.g. exams = fair	• Formative assessment, e.g. teacher judgement = biased
• Summative assessments, e.g. exams = stressful, therefore 'bad'	• Formative assessment, e.g. coursework = kinder, no stress, therefore good
• Summative assessments, e.g. exams = rigorous, therefore trustworthy	• Formative assessment, e.g. classroom observations = not quantifiable or understandable
• Good exam results = good teachers	• Formative assessment, e.g. teacher assessment = woolly and biased
• Good exam results = clever students	
• Good exam results = high expectations and choice in life	
• Grades from exams = valuable currency	
• Summative tests = error-free	
• Everyone knows what a Grade A, D, etc. means	

norm: we have new curriculum content, new ways of teaching and learning, and new approaches to assessment. Given the fact that most of us do not easily embrace change, it should be unsurprising to learn that we find it hard to adapt to new or different ways of doing something that we thought we understood. Table 0.1 presents a summary of a few binary ways in which assessments are discussed – the threads of these propositions run through the book, because such beliefs (and misguided information) are what stimulated the writing.

Politicians generally talk about specific assessments, those standardised tests and qualifications designed as preparation for work and further study. But it is time to think about parents and their role in this process, because assessment is public property. Nationally, testing is big business. For example, a GCSE in England costs about £35–£80 per subject and A levels range from £85–£160 depending on the subject (see the exam board websites for fees). The assessment business is – and should be recognised as – a social concern, because the cost of test taking in state schools in England is borne by the taxpayer (Britton *et al.*, 2020). I'm not suggesting that we bring the argument down to a purely financial view, but it does matter because this public cost is part of a wider debate about educational expectations.

Chapter 1 explains this approach and outlines my theory of a discourse of assessment and how it has evolved. In Chapter 2, I examine the public perceptions of assessment and also explain how historical, political and technical narratives have shaped the way we discuss assessment.

Chapter 3 and Chapter 4 look into the lives of those closely impacted by assessments, specifically through high-stakes tests, and consider how popular contemporary discourses have developed through channels such as social media. Chapter 5 presents some of the discourses that have explicit and implicit messages relating to assessment, such as children's literature, advertising and news media.

In Chapter 6, I revisit the idea that there is an established literature related to assessment literacy, but argue that it needs to move out of schools and into public domains, so that we can all benefit from such important knowledge. Chapter 7 concludes with my proposals for how we can – and must – improve understanding of assessment, in order to sustain public confidence in educational assessment.

The issues covered in this book are not simple, but it has been my intention to try to make them clearer for those less knowledgeable about the ins and outs of assessment. Attempting to simplify our understanding of assessment is not only futile but also rather dangerous, because it is the epitome of so-called 'fake news' in relation to the value of education. It is the prevalence of dualistic thinking about educational attainment through assessment that leads to extreme acts – such as writing to Santa for help.

1

Understanding discourse about education and assessment

This chapter establishes the concerns that motivated me to write this book: how we talk about educational assessment, and how this influences our beliefs and feelings about this crucial part of education. Such talk and these beliefs affect me, but also impact on school students, their parents, the man who runs my local shop, global news media corporations, teachers, my hairdresser and friends – all of whom have talked to me about assessment at one time or another in recent years. It is this breadth of interest that demonstrates how educational assessment is very much a central part of public life. People discussing assessment might not have a direct or current link to education or schooling, but we all know what assessment in educational settings 'looks like', because we have all experienced it. This familiarity means that we can share memories and even empathise with one another's stories.

Education is a popular topic for discussion in a range of public domains. Its role is often simultaneously prized and feared, and behind it trail a mind-blowing range of expected functions (Ball, 2017), such as:

- attaining economic growth and/or sustainability (Robertson, 2005; Cummings and Bain, 2017)
- developing an appropriately skilled workforce (Tomlinson, 2008; Billingham, 2018; Okolie *et al.*, 2019)
- providing a broad and balanced curriculum for learners (Fagg, 1990; Campbell, 1993; Ogier, 2019)
- educating students for life within and beyond compulsory education (Kairamo, 1989; Saunders, 1995; White, 2009)
- challenging and addressing broad societal deficits (Pellegrino and Hilton, 2012).

Education therefore carries a heavy burden of high expectations. The themes listed here are not exhaustive because, depending on where you seek evidence geographically, the aims of education change. They are necessarily influenced by the politics, cultural heritage and society within which they reside.

This raises the question of how education can be tailored to meet such diverse responsibilities. Perhaps it is safer – or more pragmatic – to accept that there will be occasions when it cannot do so. Supposing significant societal changes might be invoked using education, then it is logical to presume that one role of schools and colleges is to address such challenges. This, of course, puts significant pressure on schools and it influences the perceptions of both the role and value of education and schooling in society. What can happen is that the normative value of education itself becomes conflated with the narrowest of measures – test results – in an attempt to decide how changes have occurred and then whether they have been successful (or not). Even when discussions about education might start with broad contexts, such talk rapidly becomes orientated towards the minutiae of examination results. It is important to be able to assess both the value and the success of education – indeed, the only way to really understand whether learning has happened is to assess it. The framing of policies and activities is important to those who work in education and it is of value to everyone.

Before getting into the theory and practice of education and assessment, an explanation of terminology is required.

- *Assessment*: the term is used throughout the book, but focuses largely on one facet of this important practice: testing.
- *Testing*: specifically high-stakes testing, the examinations that make us or break us.
- *Students*: this means children and/or pupils, because this identifier relates more comfortably with all phases of learning, from pre-school through to university and beyond.
- *Stakeholders*: some readers might wince at the use of the term in the book, but no apologies are offered for using this very mechanistic term. Rather, it is my intention to underline two things: first, education globally is a marketplace, within which resources are bought and sold; second, within the market, the outcomes of educational experience have significant influence on the stakeholders: schools, teachers, students, parents and the public at large. Use of the word 'stakeholder' is not meant to signal agreement to the way that education is now a

marketplace, but instead to emphasise the reality of how education is constructed in our society.

- *Discourse*: in this book, I use 'discourse' as an inclusive term, covering the breadth and depth of the diverse discussions that include assessment as a discrete focus or an important feature. Using discourses to explain how we communicate ideas provides a stronger theoretical framework to characterise representations and understanding of educational assessment.

Explaining discourse(s)

Simply put, the term 'discourse' means a body of text, but text is not confined simply to *written words* on a page or screen. Texts can also be *oral* (for example, speeches or conversations), *visual* (such as a sign or an instruction), or *pictorial* (for example, an image that has a particular meaning or conveys a message), or they might be a combination of some or all of the above. Whatever their form, discourses provide a means of communicating something. It might be data, written evidence and/or knowledge. In a research context, discourses necessarily feature questions such as 'What is . . .?', 'Why is . . .?' or 'How do . . .?'. These are discourses which are defined by their inquisitive nature; they represent curiosity and, through the use of curious conversations, a need to find answers.

Discourses emerge from, and then function as, groups of statements about something, for example our beliefs about the trustworthiness of marking practices for national examinations. Over time, discourses become a part of how people describe the world. Cognitive linguist George Lakoff (1970) claimed that effective discourse comprises distinct components: it is well argued, its ideas are connected and it has structure (in other words, it is not just lots of rambling around a theme). Lakoff argued that a discourse should stand up well to scrutiny and this requires the creation and sharing of ideas that are relatable to readers. Discourses sometimes include discussions with others and those interactions can help us to make sense of our understanding of any given topic at a particular time. In essence, we create discourses to understand things such as our personal identity, our beliefs and/or our concept of our very existence. Discourses are essential to making sense of the world around us and, of course, of ourselves within it.

The philosopher Michel Foucault (1972) argued that discourses are central to the creation of personal belief systems, because individuals adapt and assimilate discourses to align with our beliefs. Central to this process is the repetition of key statements and ideas, because these quasi-mantras reinforce the validity of our beliefs and help us to continuously justify our attachment to them. Foucault (1972) proposed that discourse shapes human thinking, beliefs, behaviour and how we *live* our lives. This explanation of discourse is useful, because it provides a foundation for how we:

- make sense of the world
- operate at a personal, individual level
- operate within and beyond relational structures, for example family or local community, broader society or global society.

Creating new discourses is not easy; it requires substantial engagement. Another philosopher, Jürgen Habermas (2006), explained discourse development as a continuous process of information sifting in order to establish its value. This activity includes analysis of new information in light of prior knowledge (asking: is it useful or not?), to help us to make sense of what we see or hear and so decide to accept or reject the new discourse. This does not mean that we necessarily accept or reject something new in its entirety; rather, it is more common to take and adapt certain features in order to augment or adjust our current discourses. However, human beings are not fond of substantive change (Have *et al.*, 2018), so preparation and practice are necessary in order for people to engage with different ways of thinking about the things that matter to us.

As Potter and Wetherell (1994) explain, there is no *single* way to explore discourse; rather, we have to embrace the *complex* nature of different discourses and how they diverge and converge with one another. They caution that it is easy to be enticed by discourses as 'some analogous set of codified procedures that can be put into effect and which will lead to results' (Potter and Wetherell, 1994: 53). But this is not a logical or useful way to conceive of discourse. It is only possible to develop understanding by: first, interrogating those systems that sustain different social practices; and second, establishing how these translate into discourses characterising our sense of self and our world.

Public discourses

The definition of public discourse in this book includes communications that are spoken, broadcast, heard or published within public settings, for example through the internet, broadcasting, events and publications. In ancient Greece, public discourses took place in the forum, where orators would talk with those present and popular topics of the day were debated.

This period of history is described by communications scholars as the Talking Era (Open Textbook Library, 2016), when speech was the primary means of creating, sharing and shaping discourses through provision of information, or storytelling, or even motivating people to act or respond to the speech. Indeed, the structure of public oration comprises three general purposes: to inform, to persuade and to entertain. Sometimes it can do all three, but essentially its role is to encourage discourse.

Over time, such discourses evolved with the printed word, the evolution of public literacy, pamphleteering and the advent of newspapers, television and so on. In 1948, an American academic, Harold Lasswell, published his model of communication, summarised as: 'Who, said what, in which channel, to whom, with what effect?' (Sapienza *et al.*, 2015: 601). Lasswell's model precipitated the evolution of new ways of thinking about how human beings communicate with one another. Since the 1960s, as the field of Communication Studies grew (see, for example, McAnany, 2014), researchers have recognised how mass media influence public discourses to develop the values, social heritage and normative models of behaviour within and between societies. These influences seep into public spaces such as education. In the context of a nation state, country or jurisdiction, public discourses are generally guided by popular policies, such as legal regulations, economic structures, public services and broader social norms – all of which include hidden or implicit factors.

So, just how do we determine what is a valuable discourse at a given point in time? In acknowledging difference, it is important to acknowledge where personal preferences are situated and how they influence attempts to converse with others about a genre, an idea or an assessment within a specific context. It is also vital to understand that individual preferences will most likely be bound up with partiality towards a particular way of being and of thinking. While this is not necessarily a bad thing, it is important to be wary of how preference influences discourse with others.

Individualistic tendencies relating to the creation of discourse should also be of concern. As Scollon (2008) suggests, the ways in which stakeholders perceive their role within existing discourses make it very difficult for them to relinquish any position of power – whether it is implicit or explicit. Scollon's research found that substantial challenges to thinking and beliefs require both an openness to change and an ability to accept negotiation, in order to reframe thinking about, and contributions to, any discourse. While this sounds quite straightforward, it actually underlines how hard it can be to move arguments beyond the level of simplistic 'mud-slinging' to a place where effective and genuinely engaged discussion is possible. Therefore, it is important to think about where discourses unfold, because the situation itself is critical to the quality of debate. Given that much of our communication now takes place online, the lack of face-to-face interactions can have very particular effects on what we say and how we say it.

Online discourses

The idea of nuanced debate is hard to imagine in many environments where public discourse is commonly enacted, for example on popular news websites. Look at any news via popular online sources such as Google or the BBC, and you will find that content is followed by opportunities to comment via a blog and/or via the organisation's social media platforms. Such prospects for discourse about news of the day are appealing, as they allow immediacy in response (whereas in the past we would have to wait a week or more after writing to the editor of a newspaper).

These open forums are in fact democratising access to comment in public settings and, as Singer (2010: 281) asks: 'What could be more proper journalistic work than acting as a medium for social debate?' Online forums can perform an intrinsically democratic function, by being a space where public discourse on key issues is open to all and actively encouraged. It may appear that by allowing such freedom of expression and discourse, we are indeed providing egalitarian places where anyone may voice an opinion – in popular parlance, it is often explained as 'joining the conversation', but I'm not sure that this representation is correct. Usually, particular voices dominate and lead debates, so it is important to be cautious about claims that these spaces for discourse represent 'public' opinion. In many of the debates that occur in public spaces, the level of argument can be constrained by what Rorty (1980) termed a 'conflict of vocabularies', how one set of jargon clashes with another. This is really important in terms of how we start to think about improving understanding – and therefore confidence. The vocabulary of education, and within that, of assessment, is not always accessible or indeed interesting, but that should not negate the need for it to be understood. If we fail to find a way to improve understanding, we risk a continuation of the binary arguments that often dominate public discourses.

Sorrell (1990: 19), drawing on Rorty's ideas about 'conflicts of vocabularies', claims: 'Difference of vocabulary is a lowest common denominator; the point is [that] it may be too low when what is at issue is whether the world can decide between what is said in different vocabularies.' Sorrell is saying that we must not reduce arguments to simplistic levels that render them useless in terms of improving knowledge or influencing practice. Doing this does not serve us well; instead, it reinforces an inability to engage in potentially difficult discourses. Those discourses might be complex and conflicted, but they should continue beyond the simple 'I disagree with you, therefore you are wrong'.

Indeed, one would expect that an effective education system would help students to be proficient at analysis, effective at communication and reflective in their thinking – all critical components in discourses characterised by debate and conflicting opinions or beliefs. In order to better understand those factors, such as education, that shape our lives, we should be able to discuss them within public settings, as this offers opportunities to build confidence (or not) in them.

Confidence and trust in discourses

Contemporary discourses that challenge our beliefs about many aspects of public life have been characterised in the past decade by the term 'fake news' (Muckle, 2017; Zimdars and McLeod, 2020). The efficacy of many online discussions is also compromised by 'fake contributors' (Hern, 2017) as artificial intelligence is harnessed using bots to manipulate news and online discourses. Public discussions are at risk of being hijacked by a post-truth reconceptualisation, where personal experiences often dominate reality and ignore substantive evidence (Ball, 2017; Suiter, 2016). This change in how we evaluate the world around us has increased suspicion in expertise, while both the value and purpose of many key public services is derided (Gibson, 2018). Education is a frequently debated public service, often treated with scepticism and some apprehension, in a context where the fundamental aims of education are questioned.

It is possible to argue that measures to counter austerity caused by economic challenges across the world have fed into the fake discourses. Fear of change, fear of loss and concern about the future have all contributed to ways of perceiving society that are riddled with scepticism – this fake news has more of an impact than we might expect. Understanding fake news as a phenomenon is not straightforward; the definition is very important. Noting 'fake news' as the official 'word of the year' in 2016, the *Collins English Dictionary* describes it as: 'false, often sensational information disseminated under the guise of news reporting' (HarperCollins, n.d.). The idea of fake news is not new; it is simply that the terminology has entered a broader public context and is now used – ostensibly by politicians – to counter those who challenge their ideas.

Such behaviour is now widely documented. Research by Mihailidis and Viotty (2017) sums up the broader findings in relation to how we talk about issues of interest as being 'citizen-driven' by a 'polarized and distrustful public', who spend too much time in online spaces where they hear their ideas echoed and supported. This explanation repeats the concerns of Habermas, who claimed that people find it hard to change well-established beliefs and behaviours. There is security in the familiar, and moving out of a philosophical comfort zone is really hard to do, because adapting or changing ingrained patterns of thinking results in a state of mental disequilibrium. However, the psychologist Jean Piaget (2014) argued that it is necessary to experience a state of disequilibrium in order to learn. The state of mental dissonance might be uncomfortable, but it might also improve our condition. In educational terms, is this discomfort therefore a bad thing? Perhaps we should be encouraging it? However, in reality is it easier to engage only with materials or people that reflect our existing beliefs?

There is a cycle evident in the way that information can be misrepresented and yet keeps being promoted as a version of truth. Figure 1.1 is my starting point for an examination of public discourses and how misinformation is continually recycled and of course how this relates to educational assessment. This model is purposely broad in scope, but it is meant to replicate the ways in which speed, inaccuracy and reconstitution of errors, fake news and other erroneous 'facts' circle day-to-day discourses

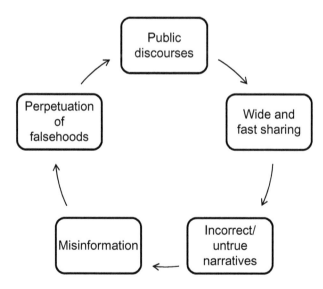

Figure 1.1   Cycle of discourses reinforcing problematic narratives.
Source: Author

out there in cyberspace and in our daily lives more generally. I urge you to think of a claim made about education – national tests are always good examples – and then run it through this model, to see where you start and where you end up.

This model derives from the discussions relating to how public conversations unfold. It draws on Manjoo (2018), whose work relates to discourses within social media, and the technical frameworks that support this medium of communication. Manjoo describes the posts, shares and responses and so on as content that feeds into 'digital echo chambers', where one community passes information to another through official links, such as sensitive information being shared between whistleblowers and journalists.

A study by Briant and Wanless (2019) explored the leaks in these echo chambers, discussing the US elections in 2016 and the difficulties in determining what was fake and what was true. Facts can be reshaped as they move from person to person both in official and informal settings. Such reshaping can distort information, either intentionally or by mistake, and when this happens, it becomes hard for individuals to believe what constitutes reality.

There are fact-checkers out there, such as Davis (2016), who lists established ways to check and interrogate claims and information made online, by conducting investigations to find reliable evidence and to challenge misinformation. Davis's website explains the nature of this undertaking as being like a detective: his work involves investigating individuals, finding credible evidence, and reading and sifting through data and resources to ascertain the reliability of sources, for example determining whether information is being spread by a human being as opposed to automated 'bots' that lurk online (Wang *et al.*, 2018; Jones, 2019). This suggests that we should be cautious about the reliability of discourses that are led by those attuned to particular forms of media in contemporary settings, for example social media managers, social media strategists and so-called influencers. Young social media influencers are important for education – and their role is discussed in Chapter 5.

Returning to the broader construction of discourses, some researchers (for example, Jensen and Walker, 2008) argue that discourses are discrete sites (or cells) to examine how individuals interact with one another, with the state and with broader frameworks of society. They call these their 'sites of social structure' and they describe them as existing within 'contests of social action'. The value of their model is in how they position different discourses alongside one another and in their enticing claim that all discourses are empty and full – empty because notions such as competition are not universals, but full once local groups/individuals populate discourse in relation to their own agendas.

Central to many contemporary educational aims is the notion that competition is a 'good thing' and that its promotion is axiomatic. Let me explain this in relation to assessment: central to education is a discourse that champions an aim of education as for enterprise, for employability, for financial success and for national economic good. This ideal is situated within a discourse of competition – you have to be the best to win the prizes. Thus, school now becomes a place where you compete. Competition is normalised to the extent that it becomes an expected human characteristic (survival of the fittest – Darwinian in nature) that is prevalent in education.

The idea of a market within the context of education therefore becomes 'taken for granted as beneficial and inevitable' (Jensen and Walker, 2008: 18). Such a claim reiterates the dominance of neoliberal discourses in education in England since the early 1980s; the language of economic markets defines such ideals, and competition is the keyword that connects many of the discourse domains together. These connections are important, because they include slippery perceptions – such as whether we think one subject is more important than another in a curriculum, or whether it is better to have examinations of knowledge set externally and awarded with grades as opposed to teacher-directed in-class assessments that result in formative or diagnostic feedback. To have useful debates that can inform public understanding will mean thinking about how to educate for assessment literacy (see Chapter 6) and where this can happen.

Where do discourses happen?

Knowing how and where to initiate or contribute to public discourse is vital to tackling the challenge of improving public understanding of education. Globally, the means of broad communication have moved from the concrete or hard copy (paper-based) to electronic formats of exchange. This has happened very quickly, so perhaps it is unsurprising that it is so challenging to keep up to date with everything that might be available in the form of information, guidance and policy. I do not spend as much time close reading information as in the past; I have learned how to skim and retrieve from the plethora of online sources at my fingertips. Generally, I am likely to seek an answer to any question using the internet accessed via a tablet or smartphone.

I am fortunate to have been born in a wealthy country with access to high-quality information resources, but globally there is a persistent inequality of access to public information. The outbreak of the COVID-19 pandemic made technological inequalities starkly visible (Berners-Lee, 2020). A United Nations report on digital development (International Telecommunications Union, 2019) makes for rather grim reading: internet access and usage is highest in European countries, with 82 per cent of individuals connected, and it is lowest in African countries, with just 28 per cent of individuals having any access to digital technology. These data reveal that there is a will to be able to use new technologies in a range of ways, including supporting education. Cheap mobile phone technologies are improving global access to the internet, and online education and digital assessments are becoming accessible, but this does not mean that people have them. There is no simple answer to this; however, noting the existence of such inequity is crucial in making sense of these discourses, wherever they reside.

The notion of communicating with an 'audience' or encouraging debate and conversation using new technologies is, argue Braun and Gillespie (2011), subject to limitations relating to the structure of new media and the speed at which we are able, indeed expected, to respond. They note that even when discourses are civil and constructive, their sheer volume can prove overwhelming to readers. News organisations are expert at what Braun and Gillespie (2011: 386) describe as: 'Containing and processing the resulting "chaos and noise," and – hopefully – turning it into something collegial and constructive'. This idea of chaos and noise interests me, because it explains how difficult it is to disentangle objective discourses from those that are either a polemic and/or abuse. Braun and Gillespie (2011: 387) found that while news sites, in particular, might welcome the inclusion of public discourses on the one hand, they are on the other hand acutely aware of just how unmanageable the 'unruly torrent of user-generated content often proves to be'. The need for some kind of moderation – or even a kind of translation of discourses based in online environments – is now a recognised fact of working life.

Discourses in education

There are many things that characterise expectations of the aims of education. In trying to understand this more, there are decisions to be made regarding what qualities are most desirable for us at an individual level, in school-level policies, through to government policymakers and beyond.

Attempting to agree what aims might be necessary is complicated because, as Harris (1999: 3) argues, 'like all matters of policy, [they] are contextual, political, normative, dynamic and contested'. This lack of an agreed definition is part of what makes education discourses both exciting and challenging. On the one hand, in most countries around the world, experience of schooling is a shared phenomenon. It is relatively easy to find similar discourses relating to experiences of being in a classroom, learning with others, learning new subjects, perceptions of teachers and so on, regardless of location. On the other hand, there are of course differences too: for example, attending a single-sex school, or how long you were able to attend school.

The importance and effectiveness of these discourses in educational settings can be appraised based on their impact – for example, on practice (as enacted in a classroom) and on individual beliefs (as interpreted by a student). Such interpretations interact with dynamics of power that are present in educational settings. As Jensen and Walker (2008) conclude, equity is at the heart of our perceptions of education. We need to have some confidence in our beliefs and know that 'the production and legitimation of a discourse (the rules about what is to be included and what is to be excluded) depend upon social and technical capital' (Jensen and Walker, 2008: 218).

Those termed 'stakeholders' in education – teachers, school leaders, students and parents – need to understand what education means to them. Within educational settings, this idea has generated a broad literature that focuses on what is termed a 'hidden curriculum' (see Jackson, 1968, for the classic text on this topic; see also further developments by Snyder, 1973). Hidden curriculums have nothing to do with textbooks and teaching resources; rather, they are the bedrock of school life – for example, how students and teachers behave, and understanding relationships with others and/or with authority (see Damla Kentli, 2009 for an excellent contemporary explanation of these theories).

A school curriculum tends to be typified as planned courses of study, often defined by discrete subjects, such as mathematics, history or art (Kelly, 2009). However, as Moore (2014) argues, defining a curriculum is complex, because definitions can range from the general to the very specific. Moore refers to Stenhouse's (1975) classic dual conceptualisation of curriculums as *intentional* – the planning for teaching and learning – and *enactment* – what actually happens in classrooms. This is critical, because the two things are continually in tension with one another due to a range of issues that impact on education policy and practice. For example, during 2020–21, schools around the world saw their curriculums, teaching, assessment and practice impacted by the COVID-19 pandemic. While school leaders and teachers were determined to continue educating their students, the actuality of experiences was varied and its success has yet to be determined. Essentially, we won't know the impact for a very long time.

Stenhouse's idea of a subject-based curriculum provides some context for the theory of the 'hidden curriculum'. It seems very important not only to recognise those discourses (and curriculums) that are visible, but also to make concerted efforts to pin down the more slippery ones. Having more information provides opportunities to better understand the development and regard for specific perceptions and positions. Subsequently, when these ideals or beliefs (call them what you will) are challenged, having more information helps us to cope with agreement, opposition or ambivalence (or a mixture of all three) on the part of others. This matters in this 'online age', when influence pursues us relentlessly.

Discourse influencers

In trying to make some sense of education discourses, one of the most important things to consider is who are the key players within and around the range of settings – from school, to home, to governance and across broader society. Figure 1.2 outlines how these discourses function – the dominant narratives start at the top and seep down to a range of stakeholders.

At the top of the figure are the key influences in education: the *human influences* (policymakers, the public and journalists), the *organisational influences* (mass media, employers and so on) and, loosely, *social influences* (governance via political trends, media reporting and discussions). These influences feed into discourses relating to all public services, but here the focus is specifically on education, and discourses trickle through layers of stakeholders.

Looking broadly at education suggests that beliefs about such key public issues are critical to how we develop arguments about policy, theory and practice in learning environments from the nursery to the university. Therefore, to stimulate meaningful discourses about education, it is worth noting that it is a broad and social activity (Stobart, 2008) and that we can only understand it by taking account of the political, social, cultural and economic contexts in which it is

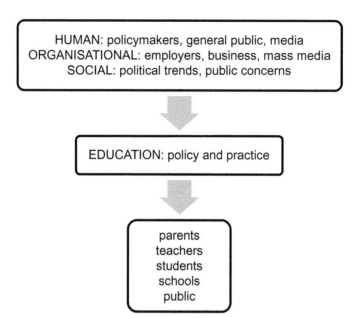

Figure 1.2   Discourse influencers. Source: Author

situated. Our responses to the sub-domain of educational assessment are subject to the wider influence of the culture and society in which we live: sometimes researchers describe this as a *sociocultural* approach to education (Esmonde and Booker, 2017). Put simply, if a sociocultural theorist were interpreting a learning situation, they would take a holistic view of a broad social setting where learning is taking place and would consider interpretations of a learner's thinking and development based on their participation in culturally structured activities in that environment.

This view of the education world presents a variety of discourses related to learning, social environments and relationships that can provide opportunities for collaboration and discourse that facilitate meaningful learning experiences. However, it is important to acknowledge that having the same learning experiences does not mean that they are necessarily shared, or experienced, in the same ways. Sociocultural theorists argue that interpreting a broad range of experiences means acknowledging the power relations that exist within and between societies. Broad cultural discourses influence everyone and frame the narratives that exist in public settings, so being aware of their existence and their composition is important for understanding education and developing confidence in it.

Assessment discourses

Assessment discourses of one kind or another are present across education literature and, whether implicit or explicit, it is politics and the attendant policymaking which generally guide the tone and the frequency with which such discourses appear in public spaces. Acknowledging the role of politics in creating educational discourses is vital because, as Broadfoot (1998) argues, they are influenced by groups who wish to direct change in ways that suit their own particular needs or desires. Such tensions are at the heart of assessment narratives. There is an added problem with a lack of understanding about the practice of educational assessment: misplaced efforts to oversimplify what is a complex process.

Attempting to outline assessment practice in a digested format is laudable in terms of broadening public reach, but the flip side of this so-called accessibility results in information that is often diluted and irrelevant. Weak information is unhelpful, because it fails to demonstrate the complexity of the issues that arise from education and how deeply engaged we have to be in order to fully understand these topics that have a profound effect on all of our lives. For example, in early years and pre-school education in England, the discourses are dominated by what Roberts-Holmes and Bradbury (2016a, 2016b) describe as a focus on school-readiness. This ideal is encapsulated in 'datafication' – the introduction of both parent and child to particular measures that summarise their educational ability. As a child progresses through primary school, the discourse shifts from play to testing, with one eye on the transition to secondary school. Once in secondary education, the discourse moves again – apparently waxing and waning with regard to assessment until Year 10, when GCSE preparation becomes the focus. The induction to these processes means that a focus on measurement becomes the norm and is an expected and accepted part of education.

Expectations seem to grow exponentially in relation to educational assessment due to the fact that the outcomes of high-stakes assessments are so influential. The book *Beyond Testing* (Gipps, 1994) resonates almost 30 years after publication: change in the view of educational assessment is needed, and this involves a systematic reorientation of policy and practice. However, despite there being some improvement in public understanding of the practice of assessment (Gardner, 2016), little has changed in terms of its role and use in our lives. The test is still king – the dominance of examinations as the international gold standard in education has created two prevailing discourses, as shown in Figure 0.1. The dual focus labels students, and Figure 1.3 characterises these labels and

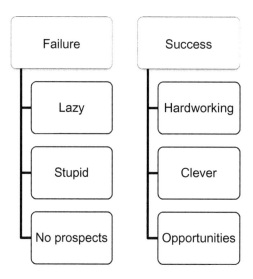

Figure 1.3   Summary of assessment outcome discourses.
Source: Author

how they unfold to reveal overly simplistic and damaging ways of thinking about achievement in education.

This characterisation is stark, but it summarises the view of educational attainments and their impact on individuals, because there are, as I will demonstrate through this book, few examples of a middle ground. Assessment discourses occur across those layers of influence explained in Figure 1.2. Just as curriculum, teaching methods and assessment vary according to the age and phase of teaching, so the discourses that surround those phases also differ, as emphasis is placed on particular issues/ideas and outcomes.

Scott (2017: 133–6) presents a discourse of examinations as a means to subjugate and control, because those that hold particular currency (for example, a university entrance test or a professional examination for certification) are a means 'to contract individuals in particular ways'. Scott suggests that this continued emphasis on test results *as* assessment has created a particular power dynamic in society that is neither fair nor transparent. In the chapters that follow, examples of dualistic approaches to assessment discourse are presented, to show how often these constrain achievement and perpetuate the promotion of ineffective ways of seeing the value of education.

The conception of particular discourses is (or should be) contested. Simply put, their characteristics are dependent upon those who are arguing for and against them within a particular setting. The prevailing discourses in education and in assessment are based upon the particular struggles and battles that are raging between key actors and stakeholders within the social field where they are operating. There are links between the discourses of education and those discourses that shape the economic and political landscapes of countries and their governance. There is no blanket mistrust of education at present, but rather the practice and discourses of key stakeholders (teachers, schools, awarding bodies, education policymakers) are tainted by misrepresentation. Reframing understanding, and improving confidence in assessment, requires engagement with the theory that informs practice – which suggests that there is some myth-busting to be done.

2
Public understanding of assessment

This chapter explores the notion of assessment in education and how measurement, analysis and reporting of results for selection or certification dominate assessment preferences and decision-making in public settings. In education at all phases and in educational settings across the world, there is a reliance on particular types of data and feedback to characterise achievement of students. Such data are, in turns, both useful and detrimental to assessment stakeholders, because the need for externally generated reassurances, checks and balances extricates outcomes from critical moments of profound learning that occur during teaching in the classroom. All of these things are assessments, so understanding what is meant when talking about this topic is vital to establishing a healthy confidence in how it is used.

As depicted in Chapter 1, concern about duality in relation to assessment discourses is neither helpful nor well founded, so types of assessment are explained alongside some key assessment theories relating to validity, reliability and the purpose of assessment in educational settings. This exploration of assessment theories includes some discussion of what might be considered extreme positions in relation to assessment of education: from those who champion examinations as 'the best way to assess' to others who oppose that idea completely.

No exploration of assessment is complete without consideration of schools/colleges as 'service providers' and how their role – and the roles of those who exist within them – is judged largely by examination results. The nature of educational accountability (James, 2017) is central to any discussion about how policies that aim to improve confidence in education can lead to scepticism about the intrinsic value of schooling, but to understand how contemporary ideas about assessment have evolved, it is important to look to the past.

Historical accounts of assessment

There are many valuable accounts of the history of educational assessment and its close relation, standards (see Nuttall, 1986; Broadfoot, 2007; Black, 2014; Baird and Gray, 2016). A full historical narrative is not the purpose of this book, but what follows demonstrates how assessment in educational contexts has evolved into its present state. All of the above authors would probably agree that the omnipresence and influence of assessment as a shaper and guide of education systems is a particularly modern phenomenon.

Studies of human civilisations from the earliest times reveal examples of educational provision as a part of the human evolutionary narrative (Harding, 2000; Lockwood, 2007; Nishiaki and Jöris, 2019). The majority of these experiences were dominated by practical pedagogies – in short, an education for life with the skills and knowledge needed to exist. Within such a framework, education is focused primarily on skills for survival, but most cultures also developed educational narratives to pass on rituals, ideas and beliefs – what we might term the more spiritual or personal. Such traditions evolved and developed globally, but a broader concept of education as an important aim for discrete societies is a relatively recent ideal. From the 1850s onwards, we see the global introduction of mass, state-funded education systems (Bagley, 1969; Green, 2013) and in their wake, the emergence of the need for assessment in order to verify the validity and quality of both teaching and learning. The desire to measure educational outcomes led to a new view of schooling and education as 'a highly specialised, professional domain' (Broadfoot, 2007: 19), reflecting the new world visions emanating from the global Industrial Revolution.

Worldwide, education systems began to emerge globally from religious and/or charitable institutions and, slowly, many nation states took on the responsibility for the schooling of their citizens. Such endeavours were not necessarily rooted in philanthropy (Crook and McCulloch, 2008; Green, 2013); governments recognised that literate populations provided an improved economic return in business. Alongside the evolution of models for state education came an interest in the nature of learning itself. This, however, was not a global phenomenon. Rather, a small number of radical thinkers, such as the American philosopher John Dewey (1910), were challenging the status quo that education was simply training for work. However, despite the rise of so-called progressive approaches to child-centred education, the research of human intelligence advocates that we can sort students into categories and scientifically measure ability (see Cianciolo, 2004 for a full historical account). In the early 1900s, two French psychologists, Alfred Binet and Theodore Simon, developed some of the earliest verbal reasoning tests, attempting to measure a child's mental age. In creating a standardised scale to measure intelligence, they claimed they could better understand its properties. Their goal thereon was to build an evidence base from what they described as 'glimpses of intelligence' to characterise the very nature of intelligence, for 'social utility' ((Binet and Simon, 1916: 183, 273). At the same time, an American researcher, Lewis Terman, eager to explore intelligence further, adapted the French scales and created the Stanford-Binet Intelligence Scales that are still in use today.

The popularity of measuring human intelligence formed the basis for new domains of exploration in educational assessment, known as 'psychometrics'. Jones and Thissen (2006) explain that early pioneers claimed that this new field of psychological measurement would be able to pinpoint an individual's intellectual capability. This is a critical moment in the history of assessment, because the idea of measuring intelligence was highly influential in the evolution of new curriculums and modern approaches to teaching and learning. There was a significant change globally in the way policymakers and educators began to plan teaching and learning. Such was the popularity of the idea of being able to measure educational achievements in a fine-grained way that testing systems, underpinned by psychometrics, flourished. This is well documented (see the National Council on Measurement, 1961; the American Educational Research Association et al., 2014).

Even more enticing was the fresh perception of assessments in education. These new approaches positioned testing as science, and they were trusted as reliable and valid means of making important decisions relating to policy and practice. As Broadfoot and Pollard (2006) explain, the element of competition within education began to evolve at this point in time, and examinations were required to check standards, to manage the outcomes and to ensure that the right people were gaining qualifications necessary to support the new aims of technological development, economic prosperity and social affluence.

Such advances hint at meritocracy, with all learners having the same opportunities to participate in competitive test taking, but in reality the focus on test-based assessments began to supplant previous forms of social hierarchy and to provide a more subtle means of stratifying societies and retaining the status quo of advantage and disadvantage. The genesis of this can be traced back to the first examinations and tests to measure recall and introduce competition into public life. McMullen's (2011) description of civil service examinations founded during the Han dynasty (206–202 BC) in China reveal a veritable swathe of tests, taken over three days and two nights in locked-down conditions – not unlike contemporary examination systems. So prestigious were the rewards for success that candidates died from exhaustion while taking the exams (Franke, 1972); they really were the original high-stakes tests, but little has changed today (*The Economist*, 2021).

Much as the history of assessment is fascinating, the concerns raised in this book refer more specifically to changes in theory and policy relating to assessment in education that have evolved since the early twenty-first century (Black, 2014). In 2021, there are many educational assessments that appear unchanged compared to their historical pre-decessors (for example, national school-leaving examinations taken in many countries around the world). In many ways, the pace of change in educational assessment is painfully slow, particularly with regard to the use of technologies, such as artificial intelligence (Richardson and Clesham, 2021). However, the use of new technologies is not part of an imagined brave new world. It is already here and is being applied in many educational settings, although the assessment landscape has yet to accept it fully. Once the COVID virus became a global pandemic, our view of assessments, particularly examinations, was forced to change signifi-cantly. This has provided not only challenges, but also exciting opportun-ities to shift the ways we think about what it means to create comparable testing systems at national and international levels.

Which assessments matter and why?

What is common to the assessments that dominate public discourses is that they are mostly summative. These are assessments that happen at the end of a course of study, for example an examination, and are about meas-uring learning or knowledge or skills (Harlen, 2008). Summative assess-ments also feature particular ways of collecting evidence that tend to be quantitative in nature – notably examinations or other tests with more discrete outcomes. Summative assessments feature most prominently in discourses about assessment, because they feature a qualification – a high-stakes outcome – that is often critically important to the learner.

There are, of course, numerous approaches to assessment in edu-cation and there is a veritable mountain of guidance (Shute, 2008; Bourke and Mentis, 2014; Black and Wiliam, 2018; Andrade *et al.*, 2019;

Clarke, 2020) on how to create, use and work with what are termed 'formative assessment processes' too. These are approaches that aim to enhance learning more substantively. Rather than encouraging students to revise and regurgitate information in a standardised, formal setting like an exam, they use a range of opportunities to engage in reflection on progress or achievement, and tend to incorporate a two-way dialogue between teacher and learner.

In the late 1990s, a theory of Assessment for Learning (AfL; see Black and Wiliam, 1998, 2018; Black *et al.*, 2003; Wiliam, 2009) emerged and quickly became well regarded as a new way to conceptualise educational assessment. Formative assessment techniques existed prior to the advent of AfL, but their status was generally undermined by a lack of evidence in terms of their educational value. AfL brought a new way of working with assessment, using techniques such as high-quality feedback (Hattie and Timperley, 2007; Hattie and Brown, 2010), student self-assessment (Dweck, 2015) and peer assessment. This is a very simplified explanation of the theory, but it is the goal of formative approaches that matter here. The gathering of evidence is not to sum up learning using a grade or mark; instead, its focus is about feeding the evidence from these activities back into the teaching and learning cycle, with the aim of supporting and encouraging the learner. Formative assessment outcomes can provide clear goals and direction but they are, by their very nature, more complex than a simple Grade B or Level 2. Therefore, it is unsurprising that we continue to focus on a proxy for educational achievement using summative assessments and their outcomes, because they are easier to understand; at face value that grade B is precise and recognisable. Summative outcomes are important, because they have a potentially significant impact on one's life, for example a job opportunity or a personal goal, and they often signify a turning point, for example the end of school or college or some other change in direction. It is surely the value attached to these types of assessment that makes them so important; they literally mean the world to us – and so might result in an increase in Santa's mailbag.

The role of education and its most prized outcomes – qualifications – can provide specific privileges. It is generally true that if you work hard and do well at school, then you can gain entry to university. The story continues that if you do well in a world-leading university, then you are more likely to be able to secure employment on graduation – but not just any work. Rather, you can be confident of accessing profitable and secure careers.

While there is some truth that hard work and education will improve your standard of living (and that of your children, if you have them), it is a rosy depiction of opportunity. Like the hidden curriculum explained in Chapter 1, there is another version of this in life beyond the school gates. The challenge of access to education is a popular narrative in fiction, for example in Thomas Hardy's heart-breaking *Jude the Obscure* (1894), where the protagonist's background thwarts his access to the dreaming spires of Oxford. Even now, despite programmes of widening participation in wealthy continents such as Europe, North America and Australia, the privileges in education and work still sit firmly with those who start off wealthy. The idea that the bright student will always find a way remains fiction.

In *The Myth of Meritocracy* Bloodworth (2016) is concerned with how assessment – in the form of exam results – matters dearly. These opportunities are not so transparently linked to merit as one might imagine. Bloodworth argues that educational privileges, similarly to other types of privilege, pass directly from parents to children and begin long before that first day at school. The lure of selection through examination for exclusive, or more academically focused, educational settings such as grammar schools has long been lauded as an egalitarian approach to providing opportunities across societies regardless of wealth. But is it enough?

A study by Osborne (2010) compared widening participation or enhanced access policies at post-16 in Scotland, England, Australia, France, Finland and Canada, and found that the success of such initiatives is challenged by social norms and financial ability. Bloodworth (2016: 83) argues, however, that this relentless sorting 'in the name of social mobility' is a common but flawed defence of what is largely a continuation of the status quo.

Even if a student from a poor family achieves the necessary grade, there is no guarantee that they can meet the next layer of requirements. My dad was an example of this – a working-class boy, who was bright and had an ambitious mother, he took an entry test and secured a place at grammar school and then university. However, the cost of university fees almost prevented his attendance in 1949 – the acceptance letter detailed costs that were equivalent to three times his father's annual salary. It was thanks to support from Manchester Corporation (via the taking of additional tests) that he was able to attend university with a grant and go on to break his family's educational mould. There are notable biographies that include the overcoming of educational adversity (Kynaston and Green, 2019), but such examples still remain relatively few and far between.

Much of the academic success from the post-war years and right up to today remains predicated on home environment (lots of books: cultural and social capital), household income (add-on support such as tutoring, outside activities) and level of parental education (being able to 'see' the example), to name but a few important variables. There is a continual lack of honesty that underpins the whole widening participation argument; while greater access to higher education for students from poorer backgrounds is vitally important, it does not provide a magic bullet. Indeed, their achievement (their assessment outcomes) is problematic, as Crawford (2014) found – they are likely to do less well overall at university, compared to their wealthier peers. The very genesis of the way we might 'measure' state education systems around the world was based on a spirit of competition; to succeed is not only personal, but also national in its importance.

Duality and assessment

All too often, descriptions of assessment in education are presented in binary terms that render any discourse simplistic and limited. In this section, I want to unpack these ideas further, because they are not simply limited to how we perceive the outcomes of assessment and their consequences for us as individuals.

Dualistic ways of thinking about assessment start well before we reach the exam hall. For example, it is common, even for experienced educators, to sum up assessment as being either summative or formative, as if these are practices that are in opposition to one another and, more importantly, are the only options open to teachers and students.

You might be forgiven for thinking that you are attending a prize-fight: in the red corner (the classroom), we have formative assessments, great for enhancing learning, but allegedly unscientific and managed by teachers (who are apparently all biased). In the blue corner (the exam hall) are the standardised, externally set and marked tests – these might be narrow in scope, but they are fair and therefore preferable. Such a bald description is not accurate and simplistically presents summative as 'good' and formative as well not bad, but 'less good'.

It is these types of discourse that mirror the success/failure discourses depicted in Figure 1.3 and, in terms of developing public confidence in assessment, they are of no help to us at all. In fact, they simply reinforce the weak discourse that lacks understanding of fundamental assessment knowledge, but also hides some of the truth behind process and practice. That truth is vital for confidence.

Is assessment valid and reliable?

To create a coherent discourse to critique the outcomes of assessment, it is vital to have some understanding of the key concepts that are central to how we use assessment in education. The most important concepts relating to the efficacy of any assessment are its validity and its reliability (Wiliam, 1993; Markus and Borsboom, 2013; Newton and Shaw, 2014). It is common for public discourses about assessment to include challenges to both validity and reliability regardless of whether the person raising such a challenge knows of the existence of these theories. However, challenges and questions are raised by key stakeholders in test-taking situations, when for example, the grades awarded fail to meet a student's expectations, or when an error occurs in a test paper. Such issues become even more significant in our assessment discourses because the personal is linked to the practice; there are human emotions mixed into the technical process of test taking and awarding. It would seem important, then, to understand those theories upon which assessment practice rests. There are very few books that explain these well to a lay person and if you wish to read more detail about test design and test taking in particular, then I would recommend Dan Koretz's (2008) *Measuring Up* and more recently Popham's (2017) *ABC of Testing*. For the sake of brevity, I outline only the key issues in assessment design: reliability and validity.

Reliability relates to assessment dependability: for example, would we get similar or the same results if a student took this test again on another occasion? The notion of validity is slightly trickier. Simply put, it is the extent to which an assessment represents what it claims to be assessing. This is perhaps the most difficult thing to explain and to comprehend because it reveals some of the blurred elements that are a part of high-stakes assessment processes. Ensuring both validity and reliability in assessments is very difficult because these are qualities that don't follow a smooth continuum. It is possible for a test to be highly reliable but not actually be valid: I might take a maths test each day and score the same each time, but if there is an error in the test paper then the test itself is unreliable and the consistency of my score becomes irrelevant. What is most important to remember is that validity is reliant on, among other things, reliability – to be sure that an assessment is valid, users need to have confidence in its composition, its application and its outcomes. Therein lies a fundamental problem – assessments are an imperfect creation of human beings; they harbour errors within their design and the attendant practices of standard setting, marking and decisions related to grading. Therefore, one of the most important discourses we should initiate is about the complex and imperfect nature of educational assessment.

When policymakers say that exams are the fairest way to test students, I feel perplexed, because logically and technically, this statement is untrue. Exams are, in some circumstances, the most appropriate way to assess knowledge or recall or competences, but they are *not* always the fairest. The notion of fairness itself is also highly problematic in relation to testing (on fairness, see Nisbet and Shaw, 2020). Our reliance on what we know is more influential than the actual evidence we have about different forms of assessment. In addition, globally there is an assessment market supported by an assessment industry and within it an equally vast amount of expertise relating to research in assessment theory and practice. This has evolved for a range of reasons, but what interests me is how it guides and feeds the reliance on particular summative assessments, namely examinations.

We seem to have reached a point where the prevailing culture in education systems globally is one that positions summative testing against assessment more generally, and it is the former that is generally privileged (Medland, 2016). This discourse is evident from the pre-school to the university, where each successive phase of education places more value on measurement of learning as opposed to promotion of learning itself (see Boud, 2000; Boud and Soler, 2016 for a good summary of these issues in higher education). David Boud's extensive research on assessment in higher education settings in Australia reveals such reliance on grading outcomes and test results that it appears impossible to encourage students to refocus their eyes away from the prize of the highest level of degree. His research team has explored attitudes to changing the focus of assessment from the point of view of both staff (Deneen and Boud, 2014) and students (Boud, 1988). What is frustrating about Boud's findings is that it is not the case that tutors and students do not know how to change assessment practices, but that they are actually *unwilling* to relinquish examinations.

In his book *Who Needs Examinations?*, the philosopher John White (2014) challenges our fascination with standardised mass testing. His main concerns relate to the ways in which our reliance on test taking is remoulding education, diluting its content and consequently reinforcing social inequalities. The small number of opportunities available to some, like my dad, will always be limited by particular variables, most of which relate to social class, income and sometimes contacts. In the final chapter of his book, White lists variables that make the process of high-stakes testing unfair. Here I have focused on three that are particularly important in relation to public confidence:

- the emphasis on terminal examinations
- paying for coaching and tutoring
- access to resources to support learning and/or exam preparation.

It is commonly argued that it is personal choice to pay for additional tuition if a parent wishes it and it is unethical to prevent people from doing this. I disagree: by all means, pay for out-of-school tutoring if it is to nurture a love of learning. But to pay solely to give a student an advantage in an examination, particularly a nationally competitive examination, is at best morally dubious and at worst divisive. Most families lack the financial resources to buy in this kind of support, or perhaps they do not know that it is available, so some students will never be taking tests from the same starting point as their tutored peers.

This issue of disadvantage is a global challenge. The income from private coaching is vast and following the COVID-19 pandemic its use grew even faster. Banning it for test preparation would potentially provoke an outcry from those involved. However, it needs to be addressed, because of the kinds of problems it causes. Here I present the case for Georgia.

Georgia's 'disappearing' teachers

In 2018, I undertook a review of national student assessment with the Organisation for Economic Co-operation and Development (OECD) in the former Soviet state of Georgia (Li et al., 2019). Georgians attend elementary schools (ages 6–12) and then basic schools (ages 12–15). At age 14, their mandatory school attendance ends and only some students will continue to secondary school (ages 15–18). State education is still very much in development, with limited resources and a lack of education for teachers. This is unsurprising given the tumultuous history in the country over the past three decades, with its focus on reconstruction and regeneration since gaining independence from the Soviet Union in 1991.

Interviews and observations with both teachers and students revealed a consistent focus on the Unified National Tests. These comprise computer-adaptive tests that provide certification and potential opportunities for further education and, if they are able to stay at school, some options to attend university. The Secondary General Examination and the Unified National Tests in Georgia comprise a very high-stakes set of educational assessments that genuinely determine the future of students. There are no opportunities to change direction or focus once a student has moved past this testing milestone.

However, the education system is evolving to focus on measurement of education and this is having two impacts: first, it focuses students on learning content only for the tests; and second, teachers will try to narrow their teaching for the tests in school, but many also admitted to spending many hours tutoring students in preparation because this private work is very well paid compared to being a classroom teacher. This market in tutoring is taking teachers from the classroom and draining the capacity of many schools, particularly those we visited in rural areas. In Georgia, those who are tutored will do well and will have more opportunities ahead of them compared to their peers, who are likely to leave education at 14 never to return.

Since 2004, the Georgian government has been making significant changes to education structures and policy, but progress is slow in a country where the population is distributed in a multitude of locations and where resource distribution is challenging. The use of assessments other than high-stakes tests as a way to consolidate and encourage learning is still a long way from being part of their approach to teaching and learning in schools. This example is replicated in other countries around the world, for example India, Australia and the USA (see OECD, 2018; Fortune Business Insights, 2021). I selected Georgia as an example here for two reasons: my personal experience of visiting; and its distinctive context as a former Soviet state. Returning to White's (2014) unfair variables, Georgia exemplifies all three: a system where summative testing *is* assessment, where tutoring is widely used to gain advantage, and where resourcing is all.

The final point is particularly important, because students in urban settings in Georgia are at a distinct advantage compared to their peers in rural areas. In rural villages it is common to have small schools with just one teacher who has to teach a wide range of age groups and who may or may not have access to resources such as books, computers and the internet. In cities, schools have better resources and more sustained connections to technology, access to the internet and more teachers. It is the context and setting for education – and then how that is aligned with the national testing regime – which reveals a lack of parity for students when the prize is the best results in a national examination.

It is important to note that even in the face of this example, I am not proposing the removal of examinations as an entity (and nor is White); rather, the system that surrounds them is what needs to be scrutinised and challenged in order to make them a fairer assessment for all. This pronouncement applies to England as well as Georgia, the USA, Canada, Australia, Singapore, France, Chile, China . . . the list goes on.

What's good about examinations as assessment?

It is easy to criticise ideas, to pick apart theories and viewpoints, so I want to state that summative assessments, specifically those high-stakes examinations we all know and love, do have meaning. There are those who feel very strongly about this. Across the public discourses, there are common themes that emerge from the claims made in relation to the value of summative assessment approaches and these are explained below.

Claim 1: Summative tests, particularly exams, are the fairest way to test educational achievement

This is a common claim but, as Nisbet and Shaw (2019) note, it really depends on how you define fairness. One of the issues challenging the public understanding of assessment is how commentators conceptualise ideas such as fairness, validity and reliability. It is possible to create a test adapted to accommodate a cohort of students and which is then administered, marked and awarded equitably, thus leading to the fairest possible outcomes, but the idea of fairness needs to be well explained.

One argument for the fairness of summative assessments is often based on an equal opportunity to compete for a university place, a job and so on. It is claimed that such approaches are fair, because they provide meritocracy through accessibility, anonymity, external marking and so on.

Perhaps most importantly, introducing students to the idea of competition via educational assessment is a valuable life lesson: there will be winners and there will be losers, so students need to learn lessons in losing.

Claim 2: Summative tests, particularly exams, are the most accurate way to measure achievement

Politicians often make this statement and it is, in some circumstances, correct. However, the answer is, like most assessments, more complex. The best way to reconceptualise this is to state that some subjects, skills, competences – it really depends what you are trying to assess – are best assessed with an examination, but others are clearly not.

The annual reports commissioned by the Office of Qualifications and Examinations Regulation (Ofqual) in England (see YouGov, 2019a, 2019b) help here – they reveal the levels of error and challenges that occur during annual examination series, and also document the public understanding of – and belief about – national tests. It is fair to propose that commitment to believing exams to be very accurate assessments is born out of shared experience of them rather than technical understanding of their efficacy. The same might be true of the next point.

Claim 3: Summative test outcomes – grades or numeric/ percentage values – are easily understood

We tend to prefer ways of consolidating information that are simple and understandable. This is unsurprising, because complicated ideas take up valuable energy and concentration. People are, generally speaking, comfortable (and happy) with what a Grade A means, and perhaps less than impressed with a score of 32 per cent. This ability to decide what constitutes success from a single measure is born out of experience and is consolidated by the previously mentioned link to competition.

This is not a new idea. There is substantial evidence that links testing to motivation to study, not least from the work of the Assessment Reform Group and University of Cambridge (2002). Examining human nature from Darwinian perspectives simply underlines our wish to succeed: we are motived to do well (most of the time) and that process is enhanced by criteria that are consistent and easy to comprehend.

Claim 4: Summative test outcomes are more valuable, perhaps even more valid, than other types of educational assessment

This idea is more problematic as, like all of the others, it is contextual too. I would concede that in some circumstances, a simple test outcome is what we want, for example in a driving test – pass or fail? Or if I am using the outcome of my test for certification or selection purposes – in a group of 100 applicants for the 20 places on my MA programme – I am looking to see who meets the baseline qualifications, before I read their application further.

It is perhaps the validity aspect of this statement that is most problematic, because it relates to the degree to which we do or don't trust teachers to assess student learning. The extent to which we believe teachers to be trustworthy in their judgements about student achievement is inextricably bound up with perceptions of value and validity. This is, of course, also influenced by what is considered 'useful' in the surrounding environment. For example, if we have an excess of workers in a sector, then the viable means of selection rests on an easily recognisable measure, for example a grade. This demonstrates how focused education systems are on a very particular prize.

Summative testing can, in some circumstances, enhance learning, but its flexibility does not make it intrinsically better than other modes of assessment. That discourse of duality has to be challenged, because we need a range of assessment approaches to adequately determine the success of education in any setting. However, there is an additional contemporary challenge, which lurks around some systems of education. This is the use of summative testing outcomes as fair measures of quality and standards in education; it is the application of exam results from individual pupils to provide new measures of accountability. This misuse of test outcomes interferes with our understanding of, and confidence in, assessment.

Using assessment practice to hold teachers and schools to account is nothing new. The system of the Revised Code of 1860, or Payment by Results (Pope, 1888), was the bane of teachers' lives in Victorian England. School funding was contingent on students passing an elementary examination, and records from the time reveal desperate measures employed to ensure that this happened. As Curtis and Boultwood (1962) explain, cheating was rife and students were coached to the extent that records document a student 'reading' from a bible that was held upside down!

In the twenty-first century, we see reincarnations of such ideas shaping the professional lives of teachers in a range of ways. These impact school resources, student perceptions of education and public views of what constitutes a good school and what it means to be a successful student.

Accountability and assessment

Standard Attainment Tests (SATs) are tests taken by all children in state schools in England at the end of Key Stage 1 (at age 6 or 7) and Key Stage 2 (the end of primary school, at age 10 or 11). They comprise three exams: Reading; Grammar, Punctuation and Spelling; and Mathematics. The tests were historically introduced as a means of documenting student progress in schools and were based on the work of assessment experts in the Task Group on Assessment Testing (Wiliam, 2001). The task group members were advocates of testing to map learning progression and use it as part of a feedback cycle to inform student learning and support teaching. To a limited extent, the SATs did do this, but they also quickly became a means of measurement used to exert pressure on schools, teachers and students. The value in SATs results became linked to teaching quality, so anxious school leaders felt forced to encourage 'teaching to the test' to guarantee good scores. It seems that they continue to do so, as the following anecdote demonstrates.

In 2017, one of my students (a primary school teacher) attended a tutorial with me to discuss his Masters dissertation focusing on the Key Stage 2 SATs. Joe (not his real name) was collecting data about SATs results and exploring the potential impact that the grades had on students' perceptions of the tests for his Masters research study. At the start of our tutorial, he confessed that he wished they didn't exist, as they had 'taken away' the usual curriculum and in its place were daily practice sessions for students. He described it as 'relentlessly depressing' because, as a skilled educator, his role had been to ensure that his students did well in the SATs, so that the school's reputation remained intact. He told me that they had done very well, but at a cost: 'SATs, SATs, SATs – that was the focus; nothing else'. Joe summarised the pressure exerted on experienced, enthusiastic teachers to subvert their practice in order to ensure that the school does well in a national test. The influence of such accountability measures is undeniable, and they are meant to demonstrate the real quality of the school and its teachers. While I don't believe that SATs can provide a clear and realistic measure, their dominance creates discourses framed by despair.

Just a short dive into the library catalogue reveals studies focusing on these kinds of pressures, in Australia (Thompson, 2010), India (Sud, 2001), Canada and Germany (Hoferichter et al., 2015), and widely across the USA. Globally, something is wrong in attitudes towards assessment and education, and yet there are few challenges to one of the central causes of this malaise. We are very good at creating, applying and processing assessment data of all kinds. It is not too overblown to state that standardised testing is often the gold standard in education systems around the world, but these tests come with caveats (Cresswell, 2000) and it is questionable how honest we are about acknowledging their shortcomings.

In terms of accountability, this means that our assessment systems are not simply a measure of individual students; they now play a leading role in defining and monitoring educational standards in schools. As we saw with the case of Joe, test results are commonly used as raw output measures for the purpose of determining good teaching – or whether one school compares favourably to a neighbouring school.

This additional layer of accountability is problematic for two reasons: first, using assessment outcomes for something other than their original purpose renders the validity of said test very dodgy; second, there is a moral imperative here – how can unreliable measures for accountability guarantee confidence in educational systems and practice?

It seems to me that misuse of assessments in this way is not only technically undesirable, but it also perpetuates a culture of misinformation about how schools function and how students learn. It compromises the extent to which we can trust our education systems.

Why does trust matter?

In conversations that I have had about how people perceive assessments, it is common for some to challenge whether trust matters to any degree. Several people have said that it is only confidence in assessment that we need, but I disagree. We need trust as well and this is why.

The terms 'confidence' and 'trust' are often applied interchangeably in general discourses that we have with one another and they are related, but they are different beasts. Confidence is similar to theories of reliability – it is assurance, based on evidence we have related to something. For example, if we know a teacher well and have confidence in them, we are less likely to consider that they would be biased when testing students. It is that experience or knowledge of someone or something that inspires confidence. Trust differs, in that it does not necessarily require an evidence base, but it can be strengthened if we already have confidence in someone or something.

We can and do trust others, even if we have no knowledge of them, so being able to trust implies a level of uncertainty and a willingness to take risks in trusting others (O'Hara, 2004). There is a need to trust our education sectors and those stakeholders who form their key players. We can gather evidence to support and engender public confidence in practices such as educational assessment, but it is also imperative that trust can be placed in teachers, school leaders, policymakers, journalists, parents and students, because they sustain the assessment discourses. If we can't trust, then it is hard to say just how we might engender confidence in our education systems.

The philosopher Onora O'Neill (2013) has championed the need to trust our assessment systems. She uses Goodhart's Law (1984) to frame her argument. Simply put, Goodhart's work in economics cautioned against reliance on emphasising the value of any specific variable as an indicator of effectiveness. His emphasis here was on using a single measure as a means to control something or anything to a fine degree. Applying this proposition to assessment is helpful, in reminding all discourse creators that once a measure becomes a target, then it ceases to have value. It is here that high-stakes tests provide substantial examples. In England, the GCSE examinations taken at age 16 are supposed to demonstrate student competency, knowledge and skills in a range of subjects, but they are also used to rank school effectiveness. However, a question that rarely arises in the public discourse on assessment is: Why do we place so much emphasis on discrete sets of numbers/grades when schools are complex, multifaceted organisations? To do so is to frame educational experiences in very reductive terms – we are back to the dualism again: good exam results equate to a good school.

This kind of simplistic thinking does not serve us well because, as O'Neill argues, making crude judgements erodes our confidence and trust in public services, and this erosion has been increasing in recent decades. There are many reasons for such destructive attitudes to thrive, but it is broadly attributed to viewing education as a market or a commodity (Biesta, 2015; Ball, 2018). Once this attitude is embedded, we begin to accept it as the norm. Once a lack of trust is pervasive, then accountability becomes its proxy. The erosion of confidence and trust in professional judgement of teachers since the early 1990s has presented a perfect opportunity to introduce a range of accountability measures by which they (and their students) are almost continuously judged. Globally, the view of teacher professionalism is scrutinised and measured, most publicly in parts of the International Large-Scale Assessments (International Association for the Evaluation of Educational Achievement, 2017), all of which comprise analysis of how teachers are viewed by parents and students.

O'Neill (2013) proposes the need for an intelligent approach to accountability; by this, she means that holding others to account is so valuable as to require only the highest-quality information and feedback that can guide and support practice. Such accountability practices would be honest in pinpointing where there are deficits and challenges, but rather than penalising those responsible, they would offer ways to improve and change. In effect, this could be summarised as encouraging a no-blame culture – as seen in some medical settings (see Elmqvist at al., 2016), where mistakes or challenges are laid bare, but the focus is on lessons learned. Such strategies model an intelligent way of using knowledge and information, and divert our attention from those simplistic measures and outcomes that appear clear on the surface but which can promote anxiety and self-doubt.

Measuring education

In England, the culture of using school test results in national examinations as a means of rating a school is a relatively new concept. There has always been a distinction between the independent sector and state schools in terms of exam results and in the expected futures of their respective cohorts of students. However, since 1989, successive governments have championed the use of exams to rate state school success as our society has changed with the growth of global competition, increased opportunities to live and work around the world and the opening up of vast economies in countries such as China and India. Continuing to base our view of national success on our economic and political importance has sealed a commitment to competitiveness. Where better to engender this idea than in schools and throughout educational opportunities?

The results of students form part of the data that rank schools in England, which led to the creation of school league tables in the late 1980s. The league tables reveal the application of market forces within education. Unlike preceding generations, students did not simply go to the school nearest to them; they had the option to apply to other schools. Applications became competitive, particularly to schools with high examination results for the GCSE and A level qualifications. This competition for school places emerged in earnest from the late 1980s onwards. Emphasis was placed on national qualification results, so that a good school (Ball and Junemann, 2012) was one that attracted lots of applicants and wielded more power in terms of attracting funding, given that it could choose the best students. Surely competition will encourage schools to strive to be the best? Of course this is the case. However, it is problematic, in that it takes examination results meant for another purpose and uses those outcomes to challenge all educational standards in schools.

Mansell (2007) demonstrated that what actually goes on in schools now is not always educationally driven: the dominant force is priming students to pass tests. 'Priming' is described by social psychologists (for example, Molden, 2014) as a phenomenon whereby a student is exposed to a particular stimulus (school ethos, peer pressure or parental ambition in this context) and this leads to the student responding to successive related stimuli. Priming is relevant here because, theoretically, it is positioned as being related to influential words and/or images – for example, in news articles about examinations it is common to see an accompanying picture of a student with their head in their hands.

As Von der Embse *et al.* (2013) propose, evidence appears to be emerging that test anxiety in students is increased when the outcome and results of said tests are highlighted as being critical to their life chances. Mansell (2007) found that students in primary schools were learning to fear a life of failure and underachievement, all based on a test. The evidence base for this kind of behaviour is revealed by studies of students who express fear of not being successful from early years education (Segool *et al.*, 2013; Bradbury and Roberts-Holmes, 2018) to secondary school (Chamberlain, 2013; Torrance, 2017) and on through higher education (Zarrin *et al.*, 2020). Ignoring such beliefs does not seem desirable in an education system designated as a global top-20 player in the World Economic Forum classfications (2018).

Any state-funded public service should be accountable to its public, but the checks and balances used to determine educational standards should reflect the very process of education itself. It is not a linear progression – there will be highs and lows, mistakes will happen, and there will be successes and challenges. But these need not be viewed as disastrous; rather, they are opportunities to move thinking in different directions, or they are a sign that something needs to change or adapt.

Such experiences would be far more beneficial to students in terms of applying their schooling to adult life and the varying employment, study and other opportunities that they will go on to have. Genuine understanding of what happens in educational settings means the potential to improve understanding of educational assessment and its outcomes. This provides routes for confidence to seep into educational thinking – and even ways of introducing discourses of trust across more public settings.

Managing expectations

The preoccupation with certification of mastery – rather than with the actual mastery of a subject or skills – is what leads to continued replication of poor assessment. This is a circular discourse in many respects: we continue to do the same things, we privilege the same things, and we can see that there are alternatives, but doing them will require a significant shift. Perhaps it is the very effort involved that prevents us from really engaging with change.

Dylan Wiliam (2016: 63) sums up the futile search for a perfect assessment as: 'Those who want to determine what works in education are doomed to fail, because in education, "What works?" is rarely the right question, for the simple reason that in education, just about everything works somewhere, and nothing works everywhere'. Wiliam's point is an important one: there are real limitations to achievement, but that should not supress creativity or a wish to do things differently. However, there are other forces at play in all education systems that guide what is taught, how it is taught and then how it is assessed. The importance of accountability and its relationship to public confidence should not be underestimated.

Views on assessment are broadly influenced by the complex nature of the discourses that encircle its development, use and outcomes. On the one hand, we want the certification and selection elements; on the other, we express dismay at the negative influences in our lives and the ways in which exam results, in particular, label our personal selves. There are some muffled claims that support a desire for different ways of using summative assessments in formative ways to support learners, yet evidence from schools reveals limited engagement with such ideas. These patterns of behaviour, and challenges to education policy and planning, are not unique to England; they are evident in many countries and jurisdictions.

Despite the ever-growing body of research on assessment theory and practice, our preference for – and application of – assessments in education settings is still limited, and betrays a lack of confidence in both the processes and outcomes of assessment. Perhaps most importantly, it is the misuse of assessment data through rigid accountability practices that continues to confound understanding of what can be important to learners and their teachers. This rather gloomy narrative points to the need to establish better expectations of just what it is we want from our assessment systems.

3
Assessment and the value of education

This chapter explores the nature of what is considered valuable in education and the changing landscape of policy reform, which has impacted on the day-to-day working of educational settings. Expectations matter, because they constantly shape our lived experiences; most of us can think of situations where our expectations have differed drastically from reality. Such experiences are not always negative, or indeed positive, and the idea of having some shared expectations of education systems is a way to explore educational assessment and the surrounding discourses.

Expectations of assessment influence how policymakers initiate change and, consequently, how educational leaders manage expectations in relation to such changes in their establishments. School leaders, teachers and students all have to deal with policy enactment and it is their responses and actions that contribute to the broader discourses relating to assessment, in particular high-stakes examinations. The cycle of discourses (see Figure 1.1) demonstrates that messages and influence from both policymaking (the political) and public discourses (the social) trickle into the minds of stakeholders. Collective and individual educational expectations are not confined to schools and students, but it is generally via these stakeholders that particular discourses can wash back into the broader, public realms such as family life. Managing those widely expressed expectations is a challenge, especially when they deviate from the lived experience.

Expected aims of education

Investing in public education is a worthwhile endeavour because, as much of the research shows (for example, Brighouse, 2006; Labaree, 2007, 2010; Schmidtz and Brighouse, 2020), education benefits us all in a broad range of ways. It's not enough to simply get lots of grades – what about human flourishing? Believing in this position is important to me, because there are intrinsic benefits to being educated that reach well beyond simply learning how to read and write, or following a curriculum comprising a range of subjects. Such things are integral to providing access to education, but they are not its sum, nor do they determine its individual or collective value. Ask people about their expectations of education and it's likely that you would receive a variety of answers. Some take a pragmatic view of education as a means of training individuals to do what we consider useful things (for example, to become a doctor or, more simply, to be literate). Others might argue for a market-driven model (see Postman, 2011) – one that positions education as a means to promote economic growth and thus engender global competitiveness. Or maybe it's more student-focused and guided by the importance of individual flourishing (Reiss and White, 2013) ahead of any financial benefits. Balancing the tensions that surround perceptions of value in education challenges school leaders and teachers, simply because they are the ones integrating constant change into their daily practice. It is important to recognise that students and their families are also affected by the constant nature of change too.

Globally, curriculums are structured in similar ways and tend to include similar suites of subjects. Just as there are many conceptions of education, there are also many views on how a curriculum should, or could, be structured – and then, how it should be assessed. Curriculum structures such as the National Curriculum in England, the provincial curriculums in Canada or the state curriculum in Chile are framed by subjects: for example, mathematics, English/French/Spanish, sciences, humanities and so on. This is important to educators because, as Deng (2020: 7) argues: 'It is content or subject matter that gives meaning and significance to teaching and learning in classroom.'

This is not some kind of pure disciplinary subject knowledge; rather, it is adapted and prepared for educational settings. One of the reasons why this happens is not simply to support teaching and learning of subjects, but also to prepare students for the assessments created to review their knowledge and understanding. These are the high-stakes tests, usually examinations, and they occur at critical points in most state education systems around the world. Such tests already sustain their own discourses related to the success (or otherwise) of individual students.

The highest of all high-stakes assessments generally take place at the end of secondary/high school and usually signify two things: a public record of understanding of a subject (White, 2014); and an approximate demonstration of how well a student has grasped their study of something. The extent to which we can determine a student's ability to grasp a subject is usually signified by a letter, or a numeric grade. For example, in the UK, GCE A levels are awarded on a scale of A*–F, with A* being the highest, whereas in China, the National Examination is scored depending on the province in which it is taken, but the average maximum score is 750 (Universities and Colleges Admissions Service, 2018).

Beyond the grades awarded, examinations of this kind signify a very important transition for students: the end of many years of schooling and the move to further education, training or employment. This is significant not simply in the change to a new part of life, but in heralding a personal identity shift – from school student to a new phase of life. Being able to understand and characterise this change is very important, because it helps to cushion what can be a difficult experience, particularly if those indicators of success that we had expected do not accompany the exit from school.

Simply put, doing poorly in high-stakes tests at the end of school can trigger personal and public discourses that direct decision-making and negative personal labelling. I know this from personal experience. This is why the ways in which we talk about assessment outcomes are critical. Poor results in tests at school can have far-reaching consequences that guide our life course, creating discourses of doom that can leave individuals unfulfilled and afraid of education. This complex discourse is initiated by policymaking, but its enactment happens in schools, where it is the job of school leaders and their staff to translate policy into practice. It is important to understand that we cannot expect parity in terms of enacting policy in schools for the simple reason that schools are not identical organisations; they have similarities, but they are not homogeneous institutions – and one problematic broad expectation is thinking that they are.

Education and the influence of assessment

As students move through the school system, they are introduced to new discourses relating to assessment. Some of these are so benign that students might not even view them as an assessment – for example, verbal feedback in class from their teacher. Other assessment experiences begin to invoke certain feelings, responses and beliefs about what is important in education and how that is positioned in relation to assessment of learning. It would be unusual, or hard even, to find an education system anywhere in the world that does not have high-stakes examinations within nationally recognised systems of assessment. This is because accreditation, selection and certification are guided by this centuries-old method of determining competence, and/or knowledge, and/or skills.

High-stakes forms of assessment can shape the very fabric of educational institutions, influencing learning behaviours as soon as the message of their importance is conveyed to students. In recent decades, this has become evident in pre-school settings, particularly in England (see Roberts-Holmes and Bradbury, 2016b; Bradbury, 2018). Research into testing and classification of students in pre-school settings has revealed that teachers 'are positioned as unwilling agents in a complex policy context' (Bradbury, 2018: 551). Although there are valid reasons for wishing to assess students across the lifetime of their schooling, what are different here are the fundamental influences of policy on schools to sort, categorise and continually account for (and count) the successes and failings of their institutions.

Holding publicly supported institutions to account is, of course, important, but there have to be sound reasons, such as: measures to guarantee student safety; ensuring that students are not indoctrinated; checking that public money is spent well; committing to keeping teachers safe at work; promoting respect; and offering a broad range of learning opportunities. These are all good reasons to verify the quality and standards of what goes on in educational institutions. However, there are unseen tensions when school leaders are required to enact policy directed by a government with teachers who might feel anxious about – or even resistant to – the value of changes. They might be unable to see just how new policies fit within or augment their existing practice, and so may view change as a negative experience. This is problematic, not only because it impacts on the professional nature and identity of teachers, but also because it is unlikely to model change positively to students. Research in New Zealand conducted by Gavin Brown (2004) provided a useful model for exploring how teachers view and interact with policy on assessment in their schools. Brown created a 65-statement survey for primary/elementary schoolteachers to assess what he termed 'Conceptions of Assessment'. His results provided a way to explain the extent to which some teachers were attached to one perception of assessment, meaning they could not enact any proposed changes. Brown's findings provide an 'assessment branch' of those discourses relating to change more generally in educational institutions. This is reflected in the vast research domain relating to change management in industry (for example, the magazine *Harvard Review of Business* provides hundreds of articles on this topic).

Employers in many sectors now invest time in understanding how to take their staff along with them and to embrace change. Change research (Trowler, 2003; Griffin et al., 2012; Deneen and Boud, 2014) consistently reveals how hard it is to accept difference and any disruption to the norm.

Anyone who has ever tried to encourage a small child to eat something new knows that frustration of constant rejection – it takes an average of 15–20 exposures to succeed (Loughborough University, 2017). Our capacity to experiment with new ideas is not dissimilar in adulthood, when we are supposed to be mature.

Brown's (2004) work is important, because he characterises the experience and view of teachers in their professional settings and this is still well used in research with teachers (see, for example, Brown and Hirschfield, 2009; Brown *et al.*, 2011; Brown, 2018). Just as all educational institutions have their own individual character, then so too do the staff who work within them. For example, we can expect a teacher in a school in New Zealand to follow the state-mandated curriculum and testing, but their actual classroom practice will always have a personal touch that relates to their identity as a teacher.

This isn't as woolly as it might sound, because teaching is not a robotic endeavour; teaching students, at any age, is not just about filling their heads with 'stuff'. Good teaching is about supporting students as learners, encouraging curiosity, challenging them and so on (there is no finite list here, by the way). Of course subjects are framed by theory and knowledge, but just regurgitating facts is not teaching, nor is it learning. There is no single formula for teaching effectively, so teachers have to employ a broad range of ideas, skills and knowledge, to work with an equally broad range of students who need at least some individualised attention to engage with their learning. On the one hand, teachers are excellent at being reflexive and responding to multiple challenges in their classroom and within the confines of their subject(s), but on the other, once they find a method that works for them, they will stick with it. This makes sense, because the implications of constantly adapting would be exhausting. As we saw during the need for fast-paced at the start of the worldwide COVID-19 pandemic, the risk of mental and physical burnout is very high (Gewin, 2021).

So, there is a balance to be had here. Brown's recommendations (adapted below from Brown, 2004) are applicable across all phases of education, because introducing a *policy change in assessment* requires three things:

- understanding of how teachers work in different phases of education
- appreciation of teachers' range of conceptions of assessment and its uses in their setting
- appropriately targeted education ['training'] to introduce and explore the policy.

Comprehending this trinity is critical to enacting change in educational assessment, because it proposes a phased approach to the introduction of new policy in a way that is not dictatorial and which aligns with how teachers work. In the final bullet, I have purposely changed Brown's use of the word 'training' to 'education', because one thing that has damaged policy enactment – and the general view of it – is the language used by policymakers and even in some schools.

Teachers need to be 'educated' into the role of practitioner and professional. It is not simply a training exercise with a formula for being a good teacher. Conversely, it is sometimes claimed, particularly by politicians, that teaching is also a craft, evoking a homespun image of the female (because it usually is) surrounded by small children, all eager to listen and learn. Both of these ideas are untrue and potentially damaging to both teachers and learners. The educational practice of teaching requires continuous professional development, in order for those involved – from school leaders, teaching staff, curriculum designers and assessment developers to policymakers and researchers – to aim for continuous improvement, even if that means managing change.

This issue is so important that it has been discussed as an issue of global concern. Eckstein (2003) argued, two decades ago, that our perception of the value and aims of education was skewed by the focus on high achievement as the privileged measure of success. Competition has skewed opportunities for advancement, and the focus rests on prioritising identification of those whose skills are economically beneficial.

Educational research into teaching and learning has developed dramatically since the late nineteenth century, but it continues to evolve, because we understand that education, like medicine, cannot stand still and imagine that it has generated a single, perfect way of working effectively. Advocating change for its own sake is not the purpose here; rather, it is time to accept that for learning, change has to happen – that is at the heart of good pedagogy and practice.

This shift not only provides potential for improvement and better understanding of teaching and learning, but it also prevents us from being blinded by some so-called educational science. A good example of this comes from the creators of Intelligence Quotient (IQ) testing (see Howe, 1997) who, in the early enthusiasm for education research at the start of the twentieth century, claimed that human intelligence and competence were fixed. We now know this conjecture not only to be wrong in terms of conceptualising learning (Block and Dworkin, 1977; Evans and

Waites, 1981), but also that there were fundamental moral issues with this way of framing human potential. The recent rejection at UCL (2021) of the work of Francis Galton and Karl Pearson's theory of eugenics – the idea that varieties of human life could be assigned different values – is a step forward. The fact that it has taken many decades for this apology to emerge demonstrates the slow pace of change in reconstruction of what is – or is not – publicly acceptable. It is gratifying to see such established norms being deconstructed as irrelevant in relation to what we know as human life.

When the discourse shifts to educational assessment, public visions remain narrow, and achievement is rarely seen as something other than a grade. Perhaps this happens because there are so many stakeholders in education and there is a need for common language about what it means to be an academic success? Or is it a means to quickly divide and conquer – for example, you did well, so exit by the gift shop; you didn't do well, so you can leave by the back door. It's time to unpack some of the discourses from the perspectives of these different actors, in order to see where, if at all, discourses in educational assessment converge or diverge.

Reviewing assessment uses and practice should signal consideration of whose interests they fulfil. The dominance of a hyper-competitive discourse of results and the continually evolving culture of comparison are not necessarily helpful to many of the key stakeholders, but acknowledging their existence is central to finding ways to shift the discourses in a more helpful direction. As Figure 1.2 (in Chapter 1) explained, there are key stakeholder groups who comment on and/or interact with assessment discourses. Exploring their different views will provide some evidence for how to challenge the more damaging discourses of duality and will also enable us to review the ways that competing expectations impact the process and practice of assessment in education. The general public and the media have more of a role of bystander or commentator, while others, including the broader assessment industry, policymakers and school leaders/schools, enact policy. Teachers and students all have to reflect on policy/practice, but it is students alone who 'perform' in a particular way and whose performance is critical not only for themselves, but also, in certain circumstances, for their teachers too.

Chapter 4 interrogates the role and perceptions of students as assessment actors, but what follows in the remainder of this chapter sets the scene for this, with some reflections on the other key players: schools, teachers, parents, the news media and the assessment industry.

What's in a school?

The way in which educational establishments actually operate cannot be explained in simple terms. A wide range of factors are at play, and when these variables are combined, they reveal unique institutions that are supposed to provide a common thing – an education. The waxing and waning of popular educational theory and practice has influenced – and continues to influence – how politicians challenge and often change key policies in education. In turn, a school's responses to policy enactment will have to take into account the complex nature of its educational community.

Marketing and promotion are now a part of educational online life. The messages that promote educational discourse are very evident on school websites, because they represent the institution's competitiveness. School leaders will have particular goals and aims for their institution, and this is where the discourses begin – the idea of a school prospectus is no longer the glossy paper booklet of yesterday. Look at a few of your local school websites and you will see that most feature an 'Ethos' tab (or similar). These pages will include descriptors such as: challenging learners, striving for excellence, creating impact, nurturing learners, promoting excellence, inspiring learners, aspiring to improve. This seems a long way from my early school motto: *Veritas*, 'truth'.

Such complex aims and ambitions for schools and colleges are very laudable and I have no problem with them. What can be problematic is how judgements of the success of such aims are presented in public settings. There is no doubt that the most common indicator of school success is its examination results – all state schools in England will refer to these, and consistently good results have significant social influences. Within this kind of measurement culture, schools and teachers become *defined* by policy (Maguire *et al.*, 2011) and the quality of their work is characterised in ways that create continual pressure and allow little room for personal innovation and/or deviation from a results-led culture of teaching. For example, in 2018, the Chief Inspector of Schools in England made a public statement (Spielman and Ofsted, 2018) claiming that the focus on GCSEs and national curriculum tests (the SATs) was stifling the teaching of a broad and rich curriculum. Such a critical statement was an unusual step for such a public figure in education. It resulted in a robust response from the Department for Education (2018), claiming that the 'best' schools offer a suitably varied curriculum, but importantly that standards were increasing across all phases of education.

Similar behaviours are noted in other countries. For example there is a growing body of research from China (for example, Harris *et al.*, 2009; Tan, 2013; Walker and Qian, 2018) that is beginning to question the way in which examination results guide school structures and learning policies. In Singapore, there have been dramatic shifts in education policy (see SEAB, n.d.) to reorientate the focus from over-testing throughout primary and secondary school and to include a single examination point per subject for each school year. Such change is significant, because Singapore is a veritable gold medallist in inter-national educational stakes, with its students consistently performing either top or in the top three nations in the Programme for International Student Assessment (PISA), Progress in International Reading Literacy Study (PIRLS) and Trends in International Mathematics and Science Study (TIMSS) tests (International Association for the Evaluation of Educational Achievement, 2017). In a somewhat surprising turn, the Minister of Education in Singapore announced a change to the national policies with the aim of 'improving the balance between the joy of learn-ing and the rigour of education' (Local News Singapore, 2018). This does not mean that they are ditching examination-led assessment systems; rather, they are refining their systems to alleviate well-documented pres-sure on schools, teachers and students. So, why is there a lack of interest in doing this elsewhere?

What do we expect from teachers?

While we more commonly align the title of 'teacher' with school-based education, in this book I mean it to cover all of those who teach – no matter what the phase or age of their students. My aim is to be purpose-fully inclusive here, so that people recognise the diverse nature of the role undertaken by those whose job it is to educate.

Depending on beliefs about the aims of education, the role of teach-ers is perceived not only as supporting students in developing as learners, but also supporting students to achieve well in gaining the currency (the qualifications) necessary for life, entering the workplace or moving on to further study – or a combination of all of these. At the heart of this is the annual measure of success: national tests. All teachers know that part of their work is guiding students towards these goals.

In simple terms, designers of national examinations seek to create tests that will mean the most able students are challenged appropriately, while offering a range of opportunities for all students to demonstrate what they know, consider and can do. This rather obvious point highlights an important tension relating to examination results as one of the many indicators holding teachers (and schools) to account: it is odd to expect more and more success (in the form of those grades) from schools, teachers and students. Ironically, this has happened in England, but when it does, it is quickly derided as falling standards. A review of the education press will reveal the phrase 'grade inflation' – too many students getting higher grades or passing exams – and rather than considering this a success, instead it is treated as suspicious and a failure of quality. Teachers really can't win.

The stress inherent in accountability and grades reshapes how teachers think about their students' – and their own – successes. It can distort reality and erode confidence in the very foundations of education as a goal/driver for public good. In extreme situations, such pressure can lead to cheating on the part of teachers, who feel compelled to subvert the system to protect themselves and their pupils. Of course, teachers are human and, like the rest of us, sometimes might make unwise choices. But such behaviours should perhaps not be startling, given some compelling arguments which claim that a culture of competition across society embeds acceptance of cheating as a part of life (Crittenden *et al.*, 2009; Kajackaite and Gneezy, 2017). In education, the blurring of what constitutes acceptable behaviour related to high-stakes assessment is reshaping our beliefs about ethics and ethical practices (Peters, 2015; Richardson and Healy, 2019). I am torn in my reactions to teachers cheating in high-stakes examinations – such behaviour is morally unacceptable, but I do feel that we should not be *surprised* when cheating is revealed. The intense scrutiny and pressure that build up in schools and colleges – where teachers feel that their job, reputation and professional future rest on test results – represent a fundamentally flawed philosophy of education.

This is not just an English problem. In Australia, for example, educational cheating is aligned with high-stakes testing and the pressure it exerts on staff and students (Ragusa and Bousfield, 2015; Education Services Australia, 2016). A countrywide survey from Klenowski and Wyatt-Smith (2012) describes events that could be called a 'discourse of desperation' in relation to test outcomes. The National Assessment Program – Literacy and Numeracy (NAPLAN) sits at the heart of this controversy. The research found evidence of schools asking students (those unlikely to do well) to stay at home during testing periods, so as to tailor a decent average result for the school. In a few instances, school principals were found to have threatened teaching staff with punitive sanctions relating to resources and promotion, and this led to teachers providing direct assistance to students during the examinations. One of the saddest aspects of this is the fact that NAPLAN is not even a strong indicator of student learning. Indeed, as Klenowski and Wyatt-Smith (2012: 75) argue, it has 'limited utility in informing the Australian people how children are learning in the curriculum'. The outcomes of NAPLAN determine that slippery notion of school effectiveness and they have nothing to do with the education of students.

In England (and most other countries that hold annual national tests for selection), there is evidence relating to teacher malpractice (Independent Commission on Examination Malpractice, 2019). This documents behaviours such as amending student work or assisting with coursework (Meadows and Black, 2018), and/or passing on papers in advance of an examination (Adams, 2017). Indeed, the issue of teacher support with coursework was deemed to be so problematic that it led to a national amendment of post-16 qualifications in 2013 and ended coursework modules, returning GCSE and GCE A level assessments to examination series at the end of a two-year course of study.

Malpractice Reports by Ofqual (2019) reveal how little cheating actually occurs annually; just 3,000 incidences of verified cheating by students in 2019, which is a small percentage of some 16 million annual entries. The annual *Perceptions Survey* (see YouGov, 2019a, 2019b, 2020) is also very enlightening in terms of how students, schools and teachers view qualifications and the key assessment practices of marking, moderation and awarding of grades. The teachers and head teachers/principals are most concerned about quality and standards of qualifications, because they are aware of the consequences once grades are awarded.

All of this points to the culture of what Ball (2001, 2003) terms 'performativity' – a characterisation of educational standards that are measured by regulation and constant judgements of performance to incentivise (result in rewards) or control (with sanctions). The point here is that performances of, say, an individual (such as a classroom teacher or school principal) or an entire organisation (such as a school or university) have become the *measures* of productivity, of meeting (or missing) a standard, to the degree that they are presented as an unqualified summary of quality or success.

The discourses that emerge in relation to assessment and teachers are characterised by uncertainty coupled with accountability. This model is fragile and reflects the broader purpose of tests judging educational input and outcomes. This leaves teachers in a continual state of flux; they might know their students best, they might be able, with sufficient resources, to educate each of their students as an individual, but all of this means little, if those final examination results don't add up.

What can we expect from students and parents?

The pressure to be a constantly high-scoring student is highlighted in online discourses patrolled by disembodied voices warning young people that they have to look a certain way and achieve the highest grades academically, or they are, in no uncertain terms, a failure. Globally, there are many educational systems based on the dynamic 'shaping' of students; this means we have moved beyond simply labelling learners as good, satisfactory and so on, to thinking about how we shape them to meet the particular needs of a society, an economy, a school and so on. Instead, their very beings are subject to intense scrutiny and comment, most of which appears to be dominated by unhealthy attitudes driven by negative, two-dimensional descriptions of how they could – or should – appear to the wider world. Such discourses are frightening and potentially damaging in the long term, so they are given fuller attention in Chapter 4.

However, parents too have bought into the idea that 'test is best'. In short, good exam results are the key to all future success, thus underlining the value of doing well in assessments. To a large extent this is true. We know that good grades in high-stakes assessments (whether from school or university) generally result in better-paid employment compared to less-qualified peers. As the most recent international comparative reports reveal (see OECD, 2020a), just being able to stay in school for a secondary education increases your earning power by almost 25 per cent compared to peers who leave earlier. Once students move onto further and higher education, the earnings gap continues to widen (a global average of approximately 62 per cent following undergraduate study). However, it should be noted that these data and outcomes are impacted by subject choice and the economic climate. The expectation might well be that success leads to great things, but the reality can be very different. So I remain concerned that great expectations can precipitate great stress, great anxiety and sometimes, the greatest of disappointments.

Of course, generally speaking, parents want the best for their children and would hope they succeed in their educational endeavours. However, there is plenty of evidence documenting where parental ambition has gone a long way past the stage of encouraging one's offspring to do well at school, college or university. Globally, research is starting to emerge which demonstrates that parents who take an interest in their child's education and who participate in school activities are modelling positive educational attitudes (see Grant and Ray, 2010; Hornby and Lafaele, 2011). In such instances, their children are likely to do well at school, to enjoy education and to retain a positive relationship with learning. I have no problem with this and would always encourage parents to be involved with their child's education.

However, I am concerned with parents who have 'sharp elbows' and who are adept at seeking privilege and additional advantage for their children regardless of the costs to others. Such parents embrace the notion of an education market and encapsulate the idea of competitive learning and assessment. Theoretically speaking, we could describe this as having social capital (Lin, 2001), or a means of accruing some kind of return on social investments. The shared factor in such attitudes and behaviours relates to one thing in educational settings: assessment outcomes, usually high-stakes school-leaving exams and the wish to ensure the highest grades possible. But at what cost?

It is, I believe, morally corrupt to buy educational benefits. By this, I mean additional tutoring specifically designed to make a student more competitive and able to hit particular grades in their school subjects – it is an economic form of cheating the system. The situation is very simple: if you happen to be from a poor background, your educational chances will always be hampered by an inability to buy additional academic advantage. By accepting such behaviour as the norm, we perpetuate disadvantage and generally continue to underpin a 'discourse of doom' – get those outstanding results or else . . . Of course, within global structures that encourage competition, it is argued that open markets are a fair way for nations and their populations to attain a good life and an improved standard of living. But in a competition there will always be losers, and reifying test results from such an early age encourages blinkered thinking: not only is that grade D or B not 'good enough', but the student might believe that they are not good enough as an individual.

In assessment theory, a great deal of work has been done to promote teaching and learning methods that support students and help them to develop resilience in relation to how they view academic success and to appreciate that grades are not the only measure (Harlen, 2008; Stobart, 2008, 2014; Dweck, 2015). The evidence for these pedagogies is strong and reveals positive outcomes, but it is subject to challenge when parents have a different view of what constitutes success. This is not meant to suggest that parents wish harm upon their children; rather, that life chances, opportunities and success signify so much, parents will do almost anything to help them. Assistance of this kind is a global phenomenon, as the following examples from India and Ghana show.

India has provided a striking example in the past decade. In a country where there are an estimated five people for any job vacancy, and where university entrance is even more competitive, then attitudes to success are commonly characterised as endemic (Safi, 2018) to such an extent that a so-called cheating network stretching across this vast country holds many families in its grip as they desperately seek ways to give their child something extra. Blatant cheating was revealed in 2015 in Bihar Province in the north-east of India. Images and video footage showed parents scaling a building in order to pass answers to those taking the tests inside – the shocking imagery (see BBC News, 2015) was shared in a matter of hours via social media streams and online news feeds and led to more than 600 candidates failing the tests. Teachers had not, it was claimed, prevented this from happening, so the response from the national and provincial departments led to increased security and monitoring of both students and their teachers. CCTV cameras in classrooms, security cordons around examination buildings, and body searches of school employees and students are now the norm.

Research in universities in Ghana (Forkuor *et al.*, 2018) revealed a range of views about what constituted cheating or even when, during an examination, it was seen as acceptable to cheat because that meant gaining improved marks and ensuring that you did not lose face. One of the key drivers here was parental reputation and a student's wish to make their family proud; students felt distinct pressure to achieve well at any cost or risk shaming their parents. A wish to challenge this behaviour has led to publication in Ghana of clear guidance on what constitutes cheating, along with further support for students to clarify acceptable practice during assessment periods.

Again, this raises the question as to why students and parents feel compelled to cheat or leverage advantage for high-stakes testing scenarios. Although it is not tolerated, we continue to treat the disease, rather than seeking to avoid its recurrence.

What can we expect from news media?

How assessment is reported in news media settings is integral to my mapping of discourses. The idea of a free press creates a broad perception that journalists are there to 'tell the truth' and to expose issues of public interest. However, there is evidence to suggest a great deal of scepticism about the efficacy, sources and validity of news reporting across all domains, including television, radio, print and online.

News media are often confined by the templates that structure how and what a journalist can report (see Warmington and Murphy, 2004, 2007; Murphy, 2013), now that we are increasingly bombarded with unfiltered news. In his book *Flat Earth News*, Nick Davies (2011) investigated the prevalence of 'churnalism', the term created by Davies to describe how time-poor journalists needing to create copy for global news media outlets rehash PR or press agency briefs. This widely shared but poorly (re)sourced news information graces the pages of many leading newspapers. Van Hout and Van Leuven (2016) argue that this has repositioned journalists, who are no longer seekers of the truth or of evidence, but instead are in some cases becoming processors of second-hand information (the fake news discussed in Chapter 2).

News media corporations are genuinely worried about the extent to which public understanding and trust in their work is viewed. The complexity of how news is written, rewritten and shared has created 'efforts to enforce certain trust enhancing practices', with the aim of sustaining a 'pluralistic and trustworthy news media ecosystem' (European Commission, 2018: 41). These are laudable goals, but not necessarily aligned with the ways in which journalists conduct their business. The very idea of fake news is problematic. It is important that this idea is understood, so that we can disentangle issues such as *misinformation* (the inadvertent distribution of false information) as opposed to *disinformation* (where the distributor has a particular intent, which might be deceitful and/or misleading).

While researching this book, I spoke to education journalists, all of whom noted two things as being fundamental to their work: first, that their primary role is to get a story that will be of interest to readers (and that will ultimately sell their publication); and second, the slippery nature of education and in particular educational assessment, both domains noted as being 'really difficult to follow and to report on', 'constantly changing' and technically complex to understand at times. One interviewee felt that there was a place for regular interaction between researchers and journalists and policymakers, to establish some clarity in reporting – not only about change to policy, but also about some of the fundamental issues in education, notably aspects of pedagogy and practice that are not common knowledge to a layperson.

In relation to assessment, there are generally specific times within most educational cycles when journalists are expected to report on key issues. It is obvious that national examination/test results will be near the top of the list, given the public interest they generate. In England, the national examinations results are released in August. This traditionally quiet time for news perhaps means that journalists will dig deeper, to try to find stories about results that deviate from the norm. Usually, the reports online and in papers are dominated by photographs of young people who are literally jumping for joy about their results, but they will also include discussion of the overall outcomes, particularly any increases or decreases in achievement at a particular grade or within a particular subject. Such reporting is important, because it is part of the public story, but it often includes suggestions/hints and mistakes that do not help with how we understand the quality, validity and trustworthiness of our current qualifications system.

Gillett's (2012, 2014) research into the newspaper discourses discussing the changes to nursing education (specifically the introduction of mandatory degree-level certification for nurses in England) found that, like school-phase education, the most pressing policy issues in healthcare mirrored those trending in spheres of public concern. Over the course of several years of study, Gillett found that reporting from the most influential journalists had some impact on the priorities and decisions of policymakers. This rather surprising finding suggests that perhaps we should be concerned when news reports are considered authentic representations of broad public opinion and, as Torrance (2017) claims, might be used as evidence to support policy changes.

However, the depth of support depends on several things, notably the political leaning of a news site and its owners and/or readers' political affiliations. Such influence can also be counter to the evidence gathered by independent researchers. For example, educational researchers (like me) might feel strongly that they have better evidence to steer or advise on changes to education policy, but such claims are often trumped by public opinion as a stronger influence, because it is more likely to be a vote winner.

This is not meant to be a cynical reflection, rather, an acceptance of part of the reality of policymaking which revolves around highly emotive matters such as education and healthcare. It seems that the popularity of particular issues that dominate the news might have less effect on policy, if it were understood more widely that sustained coverage of a particular story does not equate to a valid reflection of public opinion; rather, as Pinker (2018) argues, it contains a particular hook that sells news.

What emerges from news media reporting on educational assessment is not only the influence of policymakers on what is being reported, but also potential opportunities for policy to be influenced by its popularity with news readership. What concerns me is how the news media often report that discourse of duality in relation to national examination outcomes. On one page there are students leaping in anticipation of a bright future and on the next page are others crushed forever by failure. What is needed here is nuance. News reporting is not the place for that per se, and it has a role to play in helping to build better information and expectations, but there need to be improved interactions between the stakeholders.

What do we expect from the assessment industry?

The idea of an assessment industry somehow conjures up for me images of a production line with packages of assessment collated by pickers who box them up to send out to educational establishments and individuals. This idea creates an illusion of neatness and linearity that is not an accurate characterisation of the many organisations and individuals who are a part of the process and practice related to large-scale assessments. However, it is hard to find a better overarching term than 'industry' to encapsulate those many organisations, companies and individuals who make up the complex structures that create, deliver and evaluate educational assessment across all phases of education. These include:

- *awarding bodies/examination boards*: organisations that generally design qualifications and high-stakes tests for national education systems and for professional organisations, designing curriculum outlines for teaching, providing practice papers, providing external marking systems, awarding grades and managing post-award administration
- *test developers*: for example, individuals who create bespoke solutions for particular domains through to multinational companies that create assessments for all sorts of situations
- *expert markers and examiners*: those employed by awarding bodies to undertake marking/examining, and individuals who work as freelance experts in subject areas and so on
- *regulatory organisations*: generally, government departments or similar, whose role is to inspect and manage the quality of assessment provision – the guardians of standards
- *research and/or development*: this area of the assessment industry is very broad and ranges from academics (such as myself) to whole departments in awarding bodies/examination boards, organisations and individuals.

While not all of those involved in these domains are necessarily profit-orientated, there can be no doubt that some areas of assessment, notably national and international testing, are big business. As such, challenges to their efficacy through negative discourses relating to qualifications and testing are problematic. Recent years have seen a developing interest in how the assessment industry understands and manages those discussions that relate to the efficacy and fairness of their wares. Examples of public engagement materials are becoming more prevalent on exam board websites, for example blogs/videos to explain processes (AQA, 2021b, 2021a), or public briefings (for example, Pearson UK, 2021).

Traditionally, the discourses of challenge to the assessment industry took the form of appeals relating to grades, errors and marking. These were largely conducted behind closed doors, where the organisation/individuals debated with one another to reach a resolution. The summaries of these complaints were not secret and are generally published – see for example, the annual standards reporting in England (Standards and Testing Agency, 2021) and Australia (NSW Education Standards Authority, 2020). However, in recent years these conversations have moved into public settings on websites and social media. There is still relatively little evaluation of these online discourses on the part of the assessment industry itself and there are some pragmatic reasons for this. For example, Dhawan and Zanini (2014) caution that the online behaviour of people is not representative of their behaviours elsewhere. Systematic mining of data from social media such as Twitter (see Sutch and Klir, 2017) finds that postings are unlikely to come from a random subset of examination candidates, so cannot be viewed as representative of candidature as a whole. However, it can be claimed that social media is a valid way to listen to students – to gather perceptions and feedback related to particular features of qualifications, assessments and so on. Its prevalence is important, so the assessment industry should ensure that it pays attention to trends emerging from the public discourses that unfold on their websites and social media streams (Zappavigna, 2013).

If we view education as a business that we are buying into, then perhaps some people might wish to prosecute those within the education 'industries' for false advertising and for failing to meet trading standards. It is incumbent upon those of us who work, research and talk within the assessment world to both acknowledge and challenge poor practice, because we are aware that it happens. There is a pressing need to promote a reality of achievement that reflects success in the many ways in which it exists and the limitations of the industry to provide a perfect assessment.

The quest for credible high-stakes testing systems, particularly at a national level, that are transparent and understandable necessitates public participation, because there is a significant shortfall in how people understand the fundamental theory of assessment in education and this is reflected in their expectations. It seems that it is not simply enough for test creators to write explanatory pamphlets or websites. Those stakeholders who engage with the results – parents, teachers, students, the media and so on – all have a role to play or 'a job to do!' (Popham, 2017: 43). Part of that job description is engaging with the complex nature of assessment, to better understand both its strengths and limitations. In order to understand *why* we are assessing, we need to know *what* it is that we are attempting to assess. In terms of expectations, our changing views of assessments, their value and the consequences of assessment experiences are colouring our ability to trust them (Carless, 2009). Being able to better understand just what fitness means in a range of assessment contexts will perhaps provide a counter to the scepticism that often accompanies assessment discourses.

The next chapter examines how the rhetoric of success has skewed the aims of education, by focusing on student perceptions. The changing nature of educational institutions and the ever-increasing levels of accountability have led to a new phenomenon of students making legal claims alleging poor teaching (Gajda, 2009; Busby, 2019) and, more commonly in the USA (Taylor, 2003), claims against teachers for student exam failure. What students need and what they want is difficult to pin down. It is also hard to manage expectations, when the messages thrown at students are mixed and often conflicting. One global feature that impacts the majority of students, regardless of their age, is the access to information, both good and bad, at the mere touch of a screen or button. Keeping an accurate record of this vast data is impossible for a researcher like me, so acknowledging its presence is what matters.

4
Student experiences of assessment

This chapter focuses on perhaps the most important individuals in assessment: the students. Much of the assessment discourse that surrounds students is focused on the results derived from their education, from the nursery through to the university lecture hall and beyond. Their formalised educational existence is saturated with messages of challenge, competition and goals, some of which might be very positive and others which appear to make them fearful of never being 'good enough'. This results in letters to Santa (as we saw in the Introduction), but that is just the tip of the iceberg.

Helping students of all ages to distinguish the particular benefits of good assessment practice of all kinds, not just test results, is critical to their educational and personal well-being. It is well documented that formative assessments, specifically those focused on supporting learning, provide ways to enhance students' experiences in any classroom and they inspire motivation (Smith and Gorard, 2005; Hattie, 2007; Brown and Race, 2012).

As noted in Chapter 3, the most famous formative assessment model, Assessment for Learning (AfL), emerged from Black and Wiliam's (1998) influential publication that reviewed the English-language literature. Their conclusions back in the late 1990s were powerful and persuasive:

> formative assessment does improve learning. The gains in achievement appear to be quite considerable, and as noted earlier, among the largest ever reported for educational interventions. As an illustration of just how big these gains are, an effect size of 0.7, if it could be achieved on a nationwide scale, would be equivalent to raising the mathematics attainment score of an 'average' country like England, New Zealand or the United States into the 'top five' after the Pacific Rim countries of Singapore, Korea, Japan and Hong Kong.
>
> (Black and Wiliam, 1998: 61)

Their findings in relation to a 'top five' referenced the OECD's Programme for International Student Assessment: PISA (OECD, 2020a). PISA measures 15-year-olds' ability to use their reading, mathematics and science knowledge and skills to meet real-life challenges. The results are pored over by policymakers in participating countries as they seek ideas for improving their education systems.

Given the value of PISA as a way to frame the applicability of school curriculums in real life, what Black and Wiliam proposed was less testing (summative assessments). Instead, they argued that formative assessments had significant potential for another way of perceiving both learning and achievement in classrooms. They argued that changing the very way we apply assessment within education systems has the potential to shift students' attitudes to learning; and that it can be a lever to improve students' self-confidence, by building motivation to learn and to prize this alongside the outcomes of testing alone. Such claims have been well evidenced in the academic literature on assessment (for example, Stobart, 2008; Wyatt-Smith and Cumming, 2009; Berry, 2017). They provide some basis for challenging the binary discourses that surround test-led perceptions of assessment, the potentially detrimental impacts on student attitudes to learning, and the negative impacts on their health and well-being.

Certain types of assessment practice are powerful in distorting students' thinking in ways that are rarely positive. Getting stuck on the treadmill of always trying to be the best, or indeed trying to retain your title, has resulted in a skewed perception of educational success and, for some students, has brought about what I call 'assessment dysmorphia'. This is an homage to the theory of 'body dysmorphia' (Orbach, 2010; Mind, 2021), where an individual experiences obsessive worries about one or more perceived flaws in their physical appearance, and the flaw cannot be seen by others or appears very slight. I develop this argument to link the broader notion of personal perfection that prevails in the lives of students through their experience of advertising and promotions via websites, social media influencers and a plethora of online settings. Seemingly continuous discourses promoting continuous improvement are influencing our education systems globally, and this is not a positive authority.

Applying this proposition to how students relate to assessments, specifically high-stakes tests or examinations, is not meant to be sensational or amusing; striving for what is potentially unattainable at a personal level is reflected in other aspects of students' lives and it is damaging attitudes to, and beliefs about, assessment. The extent to which the lives of young people are now dominated by particular discourses of perfection – especially of having to look, be and perform in a narrow range of contexts – should be of deep concern. Globally, there is an epidemic of stress relating to high-stakes test taking – from European studies (Putwain *et al.*, 2016; Lotz and Sparfeldt, 2017; Donolato *et al.*, 2020) to work in schools in the Middle East (Abdollahi *et al.*, 2018), in India (Sud, 2001), across China and the Far East (Cheng *et al.*, 2014; Mok and Chan, 2016) and a very large body of research from across the USA (see Putwain, 2008; von der Embse and Hasson, 2012; von der Embse *et al.*, 2013).

Not only does this unfolding mental health crisis impact students, but it is now also widely acknowledged that teachers repeatedly report concerns about a stress-laden environment in schools. Even at home there is no escape: parents and families live with a perpetual message of the need to do 'well' in exams or expect that you will live an unfulfilled, unsuccessful life. The non-stop messaging seeps into every corner of life and while for some it can be a source of motivation, in general it is frightening and pernicious.

If it seems that negative discourse dominates this part of the book, I make no apologies for this, because it is time to face up to the problem. Attempting to characterise academic success differently might facilitate both self-trust *and* confidence in the value of assessment, and this might alleviate some of the anxiety around testing. The discussion here focuses on how to usefully support young people (and their parents, teachers, schools, society) to introduce and accept different ways to characterise educational success.

While examinations, like many other types of test, are relevant in understanding the knowledge, skills and ideas that a student can recall in particular subjects and/or situations, they do not always provide enough context to understand the student holistically, as a whole learner. This makes the reliance on test results problematic and raises questions relating to the aims of education: What do we want to know about students during different phases of education? How do students see themselves as learners?

The lives of others

Returning to that theme of expectations for a moment, we expect a lot of young people, in terms of education. International guidance from organisations such as the OECD claims that education should allow students to 'develop as a whole person, fulfil his or her potential and help shape a shared future built on the well-being of individuals, communities and the planet' (OECD, 2018: 3).

In terms of thinking ahead to life after school, the broader societal discourses reveal a future that seems rather daunting and potentially full of challenges. It is becoming clear that natural resources are not limitless and that students in school now 'will need to be responsible and empowered, placing collaboration above division, and sustainability above short-term gain' (OECD, 2018: 3). Laudable as such aims are, they are difficult to imagine in schools where the subtext of success rests on competition and high exam results.

Globally, young people face a precarious, changeable and complicated world, but there are reasons to be cheerful. Education provides very particular opportunities to guide individuals, and allows them to understand that they have options in facing challenges that confront them and deciding appropriate courses of action. However, what this process needs is continuous appraisal of what students need to know and do, and how their curriculums and assessment in all phases of education can evolve to better meet their needs.

Both within and beyond education systems, expectations are placed upon young people and these are often misplaced or unrealistic. All of our lives are intertwined with technology, whether we like it or not, and whether we purport to be technology users or not. Technology of many kinds is simply there in our lives; we are filmed on the street, what we buy is recorded, our daily lives are tracked via phones or other mobile devices – and all of this has happened within a relatively short period of time.

The term 'digital natives' is commonly applied to generations born since the mid-1990s (Prensky, 2001; Palfrey and Gasser, 2008) and has been used to describe those who have been immersed in digital technology since birth (Bennett *et al.*, 2010). Prensky's original characterisation of digital nativism described individuals who are at ease in online spaces and who use them for a range of purposes – for example sharing, communicating and interacting with others, meeting via game playing, blogging, buy/selling, and using social media. Prensky argued that digital natives learn differently from their predecessors, are stimulated by experiential learning, are adept at multitasking, and appear to prefer graphics to text-based information. However, these descriptions are now being challenged by educational researchers (for example, Margaryan *et al.*, 2011; Li and Ranieri, 2012; Ng, 2012), because digital familiarity is not always what it seems.

The 'native' description of the new millennial generations appears apt at first glance, but it is important to be cautious about creating stereotypes. Being comfortable with, or a regular user of, digital technology does not mean that users can readily transfer existing skills and confidence to educational settings. Ng's (2012) study with university students found that although it was expected that undergraduates would be comfortable using learning technologies to support and facilitate learning, in fact nearly all needed to develop new digital literacies, in order to apply prior skills in a university learning setting.

The OECD began reviewing the use of digital technologies in education in 2008 and, since then, has continued to explore this topic (for example, OECD, 2012, 2018). Findings from the OECD's global reviews and in-country reports reveal a painfully slow integration of new technologies in all phases of education, coupled with concerns that technology is distracting, which negatively challenges learning and learners. However, the ongoing reviews also note the valuable aspects of using a range of technologies to motivate and interest learners, and acknowledge the fact that competence in the use of new technologies is a critically important part of any educational curriculum as the virtual side of societies continues to grow.

Younger generations now use a range of digital platforms as an integral part of their lives. The data produced and collected from this way of life are a profitable means of advertising and driving the desire for particular items, ideas and lifestyles. It is difficult for all of us to keep up with the pace of change and, of course, there are benefits from new technologies. As the more recent OECD (2018) review notes, there is an ever-increasing percentage of young people growing up in societies with abundant access to the internet, mobile technologies, video gaming and so on. Some researchers compare such changes and access to the evolution of public radio and television in the early part of the twentieth century, and claim that there is more to be gained from new technologies. However, it is also perhaps worth considering that the way we use new technologies in the twenty-first century is very different. They are mobile, they are available 24/7, and research is revealing (Dhawan and Zanini, 2014; Aksoy, 2018; Tunc-Aksan and Akbay, 2019; Haand and Shuwang, 2020) that globally not only is their content highly addictive, but also the devices themselves (mobile phones) are viewed as necessities and no longer as a luxury item.

Devices really matter to young people. Studies from psychological healthcare settings are finding that adolescents, in particular, can develop strong attachments to their phones (Konok et al., 2016; Liu et al.,

2017; Hern, 2021) – bonds that are akin to those between human beings. This means that parting a user and their mobile phone can lead to acute psychological distress (Lian *et al.*, 2021), because this is how young people manage communications; it is their interactive norm. I can recall teenage arguments with my parents leading to frequent bans on making telephone calls to friends, mainly due to the extortionate cost of calls at that time. It is not possible to equitably align my experiences of the early 1980s with those of teenagers now, because our calls were generally to plan live meet-ups and our means of calling were fixed; we didn't carry our devices on our person, nor were telephones available as a personal device for use at any time. The 24-hour nature of mobile contemporary communications provides a way to share discourses via social media, texting, newsfeeds and websites, but this cycle is continuous. While that change in our access to information is very exciting and useful, it can also be draining and, literally, impossible to switch off (Dredge, 2018).

The prevalence of social networking in the lives of young people – and how this positions them in a competitive environment where only the right image, the best friends and the top marks will do – characterises success. This way of creating discourses means that young people create narratives, in which they carefully shape and curate their life experiences in ways that echo the competition they see in the ever-expanding world around them online. An essential part of this is characterised by their relationship with assessment and, specifically, the outcomes of high-stakes tests that feed into this self-shaping.

Discourses of doom and destiny: assessment dysmorphia

The idea that learners are shaped by experience originates in educational theory as far back as ancient Greece, but that alignment of experience and personal perception has its roots in the evolution of the psychology of learning. John Dewey (1915), the American educational psychologist and philosopher, mapped out a ground-breaking view of learners and learning in the early twentieth century. Dewey's work was, and remains, highly influential due to his proposition, unusual for the time, that schools were social spaces and that such environments could engender both educational and social reform for learners. His philosophy advocated supporting students through educational experiences designed to develop the skills required to be an active citizen.

One of Dewey's more controversial ideas relates to the relationship between teachers and learners. He argued that for students to engage with learning, it was crucial for teachers and learners to work together collaboratively to navigate the complex endeavour that is learning (Simpson *et al.*, 2005). Dewey's view was that the development of self-reliance in students is very important, because it suggests that students can use their learner identity to help them to understand both success and challenges that are a part of learning. Dewey argued that this allowed students to see a range of values inherent in both the process and the practice of learning along with the content of what they were learning too.

However, what we seem to have at present is a long way from Dewey's vision. 'Assessment dysmorphia' is my way of describing what appears to be an omnipresent need for success in educational outcomes measured by testing. It is a stark characterisation of current policies and their impact on students, but it explains the distorted view of the aims and purpose of education. It is meant to be a bleak model, because it is based on a highly constricted way of conceptualising individual value. A person with body dysmorphia is concerned with:

> some aspect of their appearance that they consider ugly, unattractive, or 'not right'. Everyone is preoccupied—thinking and worrying about their body excessively. Everyone is distressed or doesn't function as well as they might because of their preoccupation. The details differ from person to person, but the basic themes are shared by all.
>
> (Phillips, 1996: 32)

Assessment dysmorphia shares some of the body dysmorphia characteristics, but the focus is on personal perceptions relating to the outcomes of educational assessments, specifically high-stakes examinations. Therefore, I propose that an individual with assessment dysmorphia could be defined as someone who:

- is preoccupied with thinking and worrying about test results
- perceives themselves to be a success or failure based on test results
- perceives academic success as achieving the highest grades
- believes that life opportunities are determined by test results.

Students – those at the heart of the assessment discourse models – are prey to assessment dysmorphia. The policies directed by a culture of achievement that is limited by examination results are causing and maintaining this vicious cycle. Broad discourses, from the worlds they inhabit, tell students that high grades are an imperative. Their parents and families can fall prey to this way of thinking too, as the messages continuously trickle into their daily lives. Schools also reinforce the discourses of doom or destiny in their presentation of high-stakes examinations, the structuring of curriculums, focus on revision, examination practice and continual messages about how to prepare for assessments. I'm not suggesting that school leaders create these discourses maliciously; rather, they are compelled to repeat the policy edicts and, in doing so, perpetuate those ideals that encourage unrealistic expectations of educational assessment on the part of students.

These discourses are so ingrained that it is difficult to imagine how they could be changed. Indeed, there are those who don't think that we need to change such beliefs, so any attempt to modify the status quo is seen as subversion – or even as jealousy on the part of those who aren't 'achievers'. But this needs challenging, because what happens to students who don't succeed? Or who don't succeed in ways they wanted or expected? What about the idea that it's down to hard work alone, so if you fail it is your fault? Does such rhetoric render individuals as perpetual failures? The notion of failure is slippery and complex, particularly when related to educational contexts; yet it dominates the discourse of doom in assessment outcomes and it deserves some recognition.

Aiming for failure?

How we talk about failure in educational assessment is an under-discussed topic. My definition of failure in assessment is relatively simple: not meeting the standard set for passing an assessment. It is something with which I have a great deal of personal experience. I am aware of the incendiary nature of arguing for an acceptance of failure, but am concerned that the discourses around assessment set young people up to feel powerless in the face of high-stakes tests that define them.

Torrance (2017: 90) has examined the idea of how assessments define students and, most importantly, a public acceptance that: 'Passing and failing examinations not only defines individuals as educational successes and failures, but also establishes the legitimacy of the idea of being an educational success or an educational failure and all that flows from this in terms of life chances'. Torrance's argument here is very important to the proposition of assessment dysmorphia, because it is about how students' ideas of themselves are shaped by examination results. This type of discourse perpetuates the toxic cycle of narratives that lack nuanced thinking and perceptions. Such perceptions are a reflection of the dominance of binary thinking outlined in Chapter 2 in relation to assessment. This type of discourse is not new; there are interesting historical reflections on examination failure that reveal similar concerns relating to student confidence and the ruinous nature of failure.

In the mid-twentieth century, the *British Medical Journal* published an article by a medical academic, T. R. Henn (1951), who explored the reasons why some students (all men at the time) failed key examinations during their studies in medicine. Henn cited three issues: lack of capacity to work; lack of motivation/distraction; and what he termed as 'experiencing a breakdown'. Henn's paper focused on the third issue and explained that outcome was perpetuated by the fear of poor results, family pressure and, most importantly, the significance of success in relation to a student's social background. He made the important point that, while wealthier peers might be able to accommodate some failure in their academic career (whether in school or beyond), those from disadvantaged backgrounds could literally not afford to fail and this was a disastrous outcome. Henn concluded that the use of examinations for educational selection and competition was a certainty (and he was right), but added that educational establishments should think about ways to help students understand that one set of results does not determine individual capability or worth.

Unusually for the time, Henn argued that it was also the responsibility of schools and universities to help students to see through the inflexibility of many examination systems, and to understand that results are not always reflective of competence or knowledge. His writing reveals a very thoughtful approach to understanding the individual as a unique learner and, while accepting that there are times when measurement is necessary to determine a learner's progress, it is not helpful as a sole indicator of academic achievement. Perhaps most importantly, Henn championed an awareness of the danger that intense testing pressure subjects students to.

That pressure, explored by Henn some 70 years ago, has not diminished. If anything, it has increased. The students he used as his examples were mainly well-off young men, who had mostly benefited from private education; it was a foregone conclusion that they would go on to study at university. Contemporary cohorts of students are very different in terms of who attends university, but the pressure to achieve in particular ways echoes that study of the 1950s. In England, university attendance has increased significantly since Henn's time, when just 3.4 per cent of the population studied for a degree (Bolton, 2012). Over the past seven decades, a continued expansion of the sector reveals startling numbers of students: 8.4 per cent in 1970, 19.3 per cent in 1990, 33 per cent in 2000 and 50.2 per cent in 2019 (Department for Education, 2019). With over half of the adult population now participating in higher education, the challenge for graduates is notable in terms of seeking employment. It is not enough to pass a degree, given the prevalence of the qualification; students are seeking to achieve the highest grades.

Students as customers

Since 1998, the change from free access to higher education in England to the introduction of loans for both tuition and maintenance, has repositioned students as customers and therefore their expectations about the aims of higher education have changed. This is, in part, due to the significant debts (£40,280 in 2020; see Statista, 2020) incurred by students and their families, making it necessary to find well-paid employment on graduation. The high cost of higher education is not unique to England; our fees are broadly comparable to those in Australia, Japan, Chile, Canada, Korea, Norway and the USA (OECD, 2020b), making England one of the more expensive systems. However, this monetary cost of higher education study has meant that universities are expected not only to provide the teaching and learning, but also to accept some responsibility for the employment prospects of their students. This emphasis on employability has, in turn, meant that prospective students are guided in decisions about when and what to study based on a university's graduate employment records (Gedye *et al.*, 2007). Reflecting on the reframing of the role and purpose of study at undergraduate level (and beyond) now reveals that simply passing a degree is not good enough. Failure is also not an option: there is too much at stake for students both financially and personally.

Many contemporary societies are predicated on comparison, because people are engaged in attaining globally recognised measures of success, for example a 'good' job, a 'happy' relationship, long-term security, purchasing power and so on. However, such worldviews are unhelpful in terms of designing education systems and then creating policies for teaching and learning, because they channel the idea of individual success in a very particular way – and one that is grounded in slim outcomes. Indeed, research shows (Universities UK International, 2019) that graduates, on average across their lifetime, earn more than their peers who do not attend university, so this presents an attractive goal.

Alongside this enthusiasm for increased earnings and access to a 'good life', schools themselves feel the pressure of public accountability and a duty to demonstrate that they are successful institutions through the medium of high-scoring exam results in national tests. This cycle constantly reaffirms the discourse of doom: you must get the highest, the best examination or test results to be a success. Just as in university outcomes, where failure will compound students' anxiety linked to the debts hanging like albatrosses around their necks, so in schools there is a wholesale aversion to any kind of failure.

However, there are alternative views. Du Sautoy (2019) argues that schools should be encouraging students to explore and be open to learning well beyond the scope of their prescribed curriculum, because new ideas are most commonly generated at the junctions between disciplines. His final recommendation is to push hard at existing boundaries and be prepared to fail:

> Unless you are prepared to fail, you will not take the risks that will allow you to break out and create something new. This is why our education system and our business environment, both realms that abhor failure, are often terrible environments for fostering creativity. It is important to celebrate failures as much as the successes.
>
> (Du Sautoy, 2019: 17)

I am not attempting to argue that failure should be an educational goal; there is no merit in that. But I am keen to challenge how failure is viewed within the discourse of doom, because all that does is add further pressure on students to compete and to value success in limited ways. And then what is the outcome, if they are unsuccessful in meeting their great expectations?

This is why we need to talk about failure and what it means. This is already happening. In recent years, the growing literature, both in popular print and online, considers how we might develop resilience, and how people deal with challenge and failure. The award-winning podcast *How to Fail* by Elizabeth Day (2019) explores the notion of failure in daily life. In each episode, famous guests – such as authors, athletes, performers and politicians – describe examples of failure in their lives and reflect on what they learned from those events. Some of the examples are very distressing (such as addiction or loss); others are less dramatic. But all share endings that provide some insight into the particular situations cited as failures. In doing so, the podcasts expose the futility of attempting to label experiences as either failure or success, and this provides some much-needed perspective on what are simply aspects of living.

While there is little doubt that reflecting on failure and attempting to consider such experiences is insightful and potentially useful, in reality it is hard to do, because most of us are naturally risk-averse. Nevertheless, there is something else at play here – the reality of what failure looks like and the misalignment of expectations and actual outcomes. In terms of test results, this is becoming difficult to understand, as assessment dysmorphia is influencing the perception of students about what achievement looks like. What follows are two examples from my own experience. Example A is from a school, to show the influence of test outcomes on both teachers and students. Example B is from tertiary education, to demonstrate individual response and perceptions of an awarded grade.

Example A: the overriding importance of test results for schools and students

In 2009, I spent three months conducting research in a primary school with one class of 10- and 11-year-olds (Year 6 in England). It was an arts-based project and involved a weekly visit to work with the class on developing artworks and artefacts to explore different ideas about citizenship. The children were very engaged and I looked forward to the visits and seeing how their practical work was evolving. The project culminated in a gallery presentation – we photographed the work, created a PowerPoint presentation and each child talked about their work. This was a significant event, with senior staff attending the afternoon of presentations. In the break, the deputy head teacher announced that the Key Stage 2 test results had just been received and, because this class had taken the tests, she proceeded to pass around the results. Heated discussions ensued between students over their marks. From thereon, the gallery show was over. Neither the teachers nor the students were interested in the work we had done over the past eight weeks. As the discussions continued, parents began to arrive and I left.

You might be thinking: 'So what?'. I don't recall this anecdote for sympathy; rather, it is an example of how important test results are to schools. They direct teacher and student attention. We never did complete all of those presentations, so some children did not get to share their work. Most importantly, the subtle message conveyed that day was that test results matter more than the work you do in class that is 'untested'. I don't blame the school for this belief or such actions of interference – they emphasise the test-led culture and accountability focus on results.

Example B: raised expectations dashed

In 2019, I waited to hear the news of a degree result for a final-year student. Rex (not his real name) had studied at a Russell Group university and had completed a three-year degree in Philosophy; the call came and he announced an Upper Second class. My initial congratulations and cheers subsided as he quietly explained that his final score was only two marks from being a First and he was bitterly disappointed. I was quite stunned by this admission on several counts: the degree had been passed; he had enjoyed his degree; but, most importantly, his entire under-graduate experience had been suddenly discounted by the result. His attitude to three years of investment in his intellectual and academic self meant little compared to that near-miss for the highest grade. Of course, in time, he started a job he enjoyed and that grade became less relevant, but in other discussions with him since then I have found him still to feel angry at not being in the top tranche.

You might sympathise with Rex's disappointment at being close, but not close enough, to that First. It is also important to accept that in grading examinations, there are boundaries and candidates will usually fall between them. That near-miss is galling, but it reflects the reality of how we assess this kind of learning. One thing that strikes me about Rex's reaction (and I've heard plenty of anecdotes from friends who have experienced the same) is perhaps an expectation of what can be achieved at university, given the increase in degree classification outcomes.

In England, degree outcomes are classified as First class (the high-est), Upper Second, Lower Second, Third or Pass (the lowest). The recent Higher Education Statistics Agency (HESA, 2021) data on classifications for undergraduate degrees reveals that around 48 per cent of students now gain an Upper Second, but it is the results at First that are surprising. In 2010, around 15 per cent of graduates achieved the highest grade; this rose to 23 per cent by 2016; but in 2020, that percentage had risen to 35 per cent (Office for Students, 2020; HESA, 2021). Many degree courses are now less reliant on final examinations at the end of their course of study, and instead accrue credits along the way that provide an overall suggestion of your final degree classification. But there is no absolute guarantee of a particular outcome and perhaps this needs explaining more clearly for students.

Testing to destruction?

In my earlier definition of assessment dysmorphia, I referred to the issue of test anxiety and how this manifests itself in the lives of students. Test anxiety is about more than just having some 'nerves' on the day of an examination; it is a real phenomenon with definitions emanating from a range of research in the 1960s and 1970s (for example, Sarason, 1964; Hill and Sarason, 1966; Hill and Eaton, 1977; Entwisle and Hayduk, 1978). The body of work at this time was focused mainly in the USA. It proposed that general anxiety about school and educational performance can occur from as early as five years old (Hill, 1967), and becomes more pronounced as students reach key points in their schooling that are linked to specific achievement, for example transition from primary/elementary to secondary education, or school-leaving tests.

Educational anxiety is generated from specific pressures to 'do well' and this commonly starts at home, with parents focusing on their children's achievements in school (see Sarason, 1960). What often happens is that children begin to seek their parents' interest and praise, and do all they can to avoid criticism or failure. However, once students try to please their parents and teachers with good grades, this understandably introduces a higher level of stress into the situation. Simply put, that high bar is raised just a little more and suddenly it appears too far away (Zeidner, 2007; Abdollahi *et al.*, 2018). This suggests that there is a fine line between being motivated to achieve and feeling pressured – to the extent that anxiety interferes with a student's potential to work effectively in a testing situation. Like most things in education, this is not a simple idea that can be addressed easily.

Wigfield and Eccles' (1990) review of literature relating to test anxiety from 30 years ago suggested that an estimated 50 million students worldwide experienced some kind of anxiety related to test-taking and/or examination results. Their work is important research, because it proposed critical factors in understanding test anxiety that align with future self-concept of individuals as learners. Here I align this with the extent to which this supports assessment dysmorphia. Some students might be very able academically and have excellent study habits, but 'have difficulty in coping with evaluative pressure' (Wigfield and Eccles, 1990: 162).

Generally, the data suggest that anxiety is most likely to develop in those students who are not necessarily high-achievers and who hold a fixed view of their potential. It seems that this willingness to keep a firm hold of one's early self-perception of ability as immovable leads to students believing that they do not – and will not – have the capacity to succeed where they once have failed or improve what they consider to be poor or average achievement. Looking to the future, this is valuable information, because it suggests that a dysmorphic view of ability will be transported beyond school. Not only is a student who suffers with test anxiety likely to underestimate themselves in terms of exam outcomes, but they are also potentially likely to allow this view to guide decision-making in relation to further education of any kind.

Over the past two decades in England, David Putwain's work (for example, Putwain, 2008; Putwain et al., 2016; Putwain and von der Embse, 2018) provides a significant body of evidence for constructing a detailed view of test anxiety. He noted that prior to the late 1980s, there were few studies about test anxiety in England. However, the significant changes in assessment policy and practice integral to the 1988 Education Reform Act (Black, 1988; Nebesnuick, 1990) changed this – notably, students became students units, rendering them less than human. The introduction of a National Curriculum with aligned systems of assessments throughout a student's schooling heralded a new approach to state education in England, and the publication of assessment results in league tables changed the public perception of success in education significantly (Reay and Wiliam, 1999; Perryman et al., 2011). This was the advent of schools in competition with one another. National test results were a significant part of this, so students played a key role in determining the success (or otherwise) of their school.

Putwain's work is mostly focused on England, but his findings resonate globally through discourses surrounding the International Large-Scale Assessments (ILSA): PISA, TIMSS and PIRLS (OECD, 2017). He reiterates the claims of those who posit that the power of accountability measures in schools has skewed not just how teachers have to teach, but also the value of nationally recognised qualifications such as GCSEs and A levels. His research (Putwain and Daly, 2014) has found evidence that some students view all assessment-focused educational situations as threatening and find it very hard to change ingrained patterns of response that are underpinned by the assessment dysmorphia definition that your very life success is based on doing well in tests.

The OECD's (2017) report on stress for school-age children cites a feeling of pressure to get good grades as being critically important for the majority of young people. Despite many studies (Hembree, 1988; McDonald, 2001; Von de Embse et al., 2013) demonstrating the negative impact of both schoolwork-related anxiety and test anxiety on both academic performance and general well-being, we continue to plan, deliver and assess education in the same way. As students move into the later years of schooling, the academic demands on them increase and they are expected to manage this along with their emotional responses to it.

This perpetual cycle of assessment stress is exemplified in the International PISA (OECD, 2020a) and TIMSS/PIRLS (https://www.iea.nl/) tests. These global, comparative tests not only examine data from tests sat in schools in participating countries, but also collate social data relating to student and teacher experiences. PISA surveys (for 15-year-olds) collect data about student well-being; in the last two cycles in 2015 and 2018 (OECD, 2015, 2019) PISA surveys found that more than half of all student participants admitted to being stressed about testing and examinations. The 2015 survey found that 59 per cent of students were concerned about test difficulty and 66 per cent repeatedly worried about achieving poor grades; of these, girls (64 per cent) reported greater levels of anxiety than boys (47 per cent).

Echoing these findings, TIMSS 2019 (Richardson *et al.*, 2020) found that despite doing well in the mathematics and science tests, girls in England still felt a lack of confidence in their ability to achieve well in examinations. Research into student confidence and test anxiety, based on a review of global studies including data from England, the Netherlands, Japan, Kenya and the USA (D'Agostino *et al.*, 2021), reveals a consistent pattern of student anxiety about testing and test results: girls consistently demonstrate higher rates of test anxiety, and overall, students who perform well tend to be more concerned about test outcomes compared to their peers. So what does this tell us?

Our understanding of test anxiety and how it impacts young people matters, because it is not something that exists in a vacuum. In August 2017, Coates and Lay (2018: 1) reported on multiple researches from the Royal College of Psychiatrists that claimed a range of factors were placing intolerable pressure on young children. Top of the list were 'academic pressures and exam pressures'. An investigation conducted by journalists from *The Times* newspaper (Coates and Lay, 2018) found that reported incidents of self-harm among school-age students had doubled between 2012 and 2018, with more than 70,000 children admitting to using self-harm to relieve stress. Of course, not all of these incidences can be attributed to assessment pressures, but it is notable that examinations are regularly cited by organisations that support young people (for example, Nugent *et al.*, 2015; James, 2017; YoungMinds, 2017; Papamichail and Sharma, 2019).

One of the more unsavoury aspects of recent public discourses surrounding young people has been the prevalence of the derogatory term 'snowflake' to describe the millennial generation – those existing at the heart of the national testing systems (*The Economist*, 2016; Smith, 2018). It is defined as: 'Originally and chiefly U.S. . . . a person mockingly characterized as overly sensitive or easily offended, one said to consider himself/herself entitled to special treatment or consideration' (*Oxford English Dictionary*, n.d.). This term is widely, and often unfairly, used in the media (Almog and Almog, 2019) in relation to students' responses to the challenges they face in educational settings. This negates the pressure resulting from the way that assessment outcomes are reified and dominant in their day-to-day lives. Linguistic analysis of terms such as 'snowflake' describes them as manipulative and even 'dehumanising metaphors [that] make use of inanimate imagery in order to denigrate a person or a group of people' (Prażmo, 2019).

Paying attention to the anxiety that accompanies the test and assessment experience for many young people requires a commitment to understanding – and to pushing back against – such negative responses that attempt to belittle the lived experience for students who are exhibiting symptoms of assessment dysmorphia. In the past, the stress related to assessment may have been the topic of conversation in the months prior to national examinations (usually April and May). Now the pressure continues to peak around main examination periods, but constantly feeds into the school system on a daily basis, so that there is a year-round pressure relating to revision, preparation and focusing on high-stakes assessment. Perpetuating attempts to measure the unmeasurable continues to nourish the prevalence of assessment dysmorphia. All students deserve better, but to address and 'treat' assessment dysmorphia will require attention to the sources that perpetuate unhelpful messages.

In Chapter 5, the ways that assessment dysmorphia feeds into particular discourses (such as print, news and social media) will be presented, and examples of a range of symbolic discourses, including imagery, will help to explore the ways in which we create, share and preserve assessment discourses.

5
Depicting assessment in public places

Words are powerful tools to explain perception. Both text and imagery can feed into and shape the nature of discourses and, in doing so, determine how they feed into our day-to-day lives. Assessment is represented in a range of public spaces and these depictions create discourses that are then reshaped and reproduced by the many stakeholders who interact with them. Given the popularity of social media, it is perhaps unsurprising that there are plenty of examples to be drawn from the online lives of others. I have already established the importance of social media spaces in society and their role in the lives of students, but it does not end there. From children's literature to news media there are images and visual cues initiating and sustaining public discourses focused on the value of education and the role of assessment. In this chapter, I explore just a few examples.

There are particular methods devoted to analysis of imagery (for example, Bauer and Gaskell, 2000; Atkinson, 2012, 2018), and they build on the well-established ideas about human beings having multiple ways of seeing ourselves and our societies. For example, in the early 1970s, John Berger's BBC programme based on his book *Ways of Seeing* (Berger, 2008) challenged how we look at the world – specifically, how the way that visual arts and media represent our societies, politics and culture. His work was ground-breaking, because he argued that we create unique interpretations of our existence in the world. We make choices about what we deem to be valuable. Indeed, his claim that 'we only see what we look at. To look is an act of choice' (Berger, 1972: 9) is useful in foregrounding the issues in this chapter.

Shared visual media influences discourses about educational assessment, and this is something that students engage with. Understanding this engagement matters because, as I will propose, images can serve as a pretext for exploring key social concepts. As we view our worlds, we also evolve particular competences that allow us to be spectators who are not simply receiving messages, but also becoming critical and participative viewers. However, these kinds of activity require engagement (Richardson *et al.*, 2020) and this involves a systematic approach to interpretation, in order to identify the potential power of artworks (no matter what format they take). Once we can do this, we can become adept at recognising the multiple codes that are a part of creative artworks. We can then use such codes to explore ideas.

Experts who conduct research into visual media (for example, Pink, 2007) have created methods of analysis to explore how visual messages in media such as photography, social media and/or newspapers are read, understood and interpreted – and, importantly, the extent to which they might have an impact on viewers. However, absolute proof of impact is difficult to measure. So my point here is to highlight the way that messages might infiltrate our daily lives and to suggest that we be aware of this and of its potential to influence our feelings about education and, more specifically, about assessment.

Noticing codification or subtle messaging provides an opportunity to consider how it might impact on students and/or on a wider public conception of what is understood about assessment. I began collecting imagery relating to assessment some years ago and have categorised images thematically. In what follows, I align these categories with the discourses (see Figure 5.1).

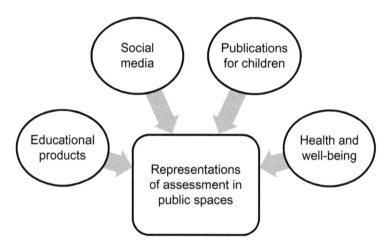

Figure 5.1   Representations of assessment in public spaces.
Source: Author

I will start by presenting examples of assessment discourses where students (and their parents) are targeted as consumers of education and of the outcomes of education, specifically examination results. Some of the public spaces where educational assessment raises its head are surprising, for example on supermarket shelves or in public health messaging. Other contexts are perhaps more obvious, such as in bookshops and on social media. The locations themselves present a broad range of themes. My aim is to highlight their existence, as opportunities to steer assessment discourses in particular ways.

The dominance of social media in public spaces is a core focus for this chapter, but it is not my intention to demonise social media. That would be too easy and too simplistic, particularly as I'm an avid user of Twitter and a fan of its value in sharing and supporting research. However, the way that messages spread through social media channels seems to have a profound effect on the types of discourse that dominate how assessment processes and outcomes are characterised in a very public and uncontrolled space. Against this background, the use of social media acquires a particular importance relating to how educational discourses are managed, both by organisations and by individuals.

Returning to the theme of duality, this chapter explores the extent to which misinformation is tackled – and how, due to the speed and frequency with which information is posted, shared and distributed, errors are corrected (or not). We need to decide what success looks like, and perhaps more importantly, to accept that it can take a range of divergent and fluctuating themes.

Education products

I have already acknowledged that education is part of the broad global 'market' (Ball and Junemann, 2012), where the provider (the policymakers and the institution) offers its goods to a customer base (the public). It has not always been the case, but the changes brought about by globalisation in the latter part of the twentieth century saw many public services, including education, literally up for sale (Stromquist, 2002; Robertson, 2005; Amaral *et al.*, 2019). This change has impacted on all phases of education – from universities (Molesworth *et al.*, 2011) to all ages of school-based education (Maxwell *et al.*, 2018). While it is claimed that this model drives up standards through competition, it is not without flaws.

Furedi (2010: 2) explains that applying a markets model to education means that schools function not only as economic entities, but settle into a particular political and ideological process that is focused on efficiency, economics and always aiming to win. It is important that we recognise the effect that this has on how education systems function and, in particular, which aspects of educational policy and practice have seen significant influence from external stakeholders.

In this context, the role of assessment too has been marketised. It is a genuinely global business that includes:

- test development
- curriculum development
- marking
- awarding processes
- qualification-linked teaching and learning resources.

Within the confines of an assessment-heavy model of education, there is money to be made. So the focus of the providers rests on the perceived needs of the public – in this case, the need for 'good' qualifications that indicate success in education. The stakes for these goals are high, because they can enhance quality of life and access of opportunity. Their value is promoted in ways that may seem surprising, when presented as they are here.

Read all about it: the value of educational publications

The global market for so-called 'educational publications' – those with few advertisements or no advertising, those with no links to specific characters from film or television, and those that include subject-focused content, for example science experiments – is very lucrative (The School Reading List, 2021). It is becoming saturated from pre-school to teenagers and beyond. E-books and online magazines are one key market, but there is still a lucrative trade in physical items. These are no longer just sold in bookshops or newsagents; it is possible to pick up a revision guide for SATs in England along with your weekly shop in any major supermarket. The sales of revision or practice guides for high-stakes testing have never been so buoyant.

Over the past decade, changes to bookshops have demonstrated the popularity of test preparation literature. This often has its own section of

Figure 5.2 Children's department in an English bookshop.
Source: Author

the shop floor, which is very different from the reading section. I've noted layouts of bookshops in a range of countries, including in Europe, the USA, Canada and Asia. The children's section of a bookshop is usually beautifully decorated and features low tables, book boxes, cushions and toys. See Figure 5.2, a photo taken in my local independent bookshop in England – this is typical of a children's area. These features are designed to make children want to stay and handle the goods; this, in itself, is no bad thing.

This setting does everything we might wish to encourage young people to engage with books and reading. Contrast this with signage in other booksellers, including one in London where readers are directed to 'Children' or to 'Education'. It's in the latter department where things change. Here, books are shelved with few accessories to entice the reader to while away an hour; rather, the focus is almost exclusively on revision guides and test preparation materials from the start of school right through to post-16 phases of schooling.

The same can be found on booksellers' websites too. Following the filter for 'Education' under the 'Children's' tab on the popular UK bookshop Waterstones leads to further tabs arranged by age but notably by test-type too. The first book cover images seen are all related to test taking under the heading 'Our Best Learning & Education Books'. To me, there is a simple message here: *Education* is about taking tests, but other reading is for fun. Perhaps this conclusion is not the intention of the bookshops, and I'm sure that their marketing departments are not specifically guiding readers to this end. However, there is a huge global market for test preparation and revision resources. I can't prove that such displays will influence how young people and their parents will perceive the purpose of education, but they suggest implicit associations of what the publishing industry might term as 'educational' and it is linked to testing.

This is big business. In fact, it is such big business that none of the UK's major publishing groups would even divulge to me for the purposes of this research the proportion of their market that is made up of revision/test practice sales. However, recent research from India (Khaitan *et al.*, 2017) reveals that increased sales of test preparation materials across all phases of education in India are valued at US$515 million dollars. What is striking about this sum is the increased value over just five years – from US$43 million in 2016. This characterises the incredible value and importance of this market. The research coming from India reveals the constant race for attaining an education and passing the high-stakes tests, because they can, as discussed in Chapter 3, provide a potential ladder out of poverty.

In terms of my scrutiny of symbolic messaging in public settings, there is something here that aligns with: the seriousness of testing and its results; and a definition of education as a measureable entity. It is not only in bookshops that we find revision and cramming guides for tests – they are a permanent feature on the news/magazine shelves of shops and supermarkets too. They sit alongside the more entertaining or casual reading for young people, perhaps providing a reminder for both students and their parents of what else the students could be doing, instead of trying the latest blusher or reviewing the best online gaming. There is no escape from the tyranny of the test.

Here, it is important to return to the earlier theme of priming (see Chapter 2), because retailers need to make money. They invest heavily in layout and displays that encourage particular purchasing behaviours. This ensures that consumers are prompted to think about what is on offer and understand its purpose and context – the informal versus the 'educational'. While we might categorise children's literature as more informal, there is plenty of signalling about formal assessments and high-stakes testing in popular fiction around the world. The pressure of testing inspires authors to write on these issues and, as the next section explores, there are some publications that appear to tread a fine line between challenging test cultures and promoting their value.

Assessment in children's literature

Within the field of children's literature, school has been – and continues to be – a popular theme (Woodward-Smith, 2011; Pesold, 2017). Globally, this narrative prevails because it is something with which most children readily identify (see for example, Butler and Reynolds, 2014). The way in which school features in children's literature is also dependent upon the particular genre of the book and/or book series. There are instances where school features as a part of narrative, but is not the focus of the overall story. For example, in Roald Dahl's *Matilda* (1988), the protagonist is a highly able child, who outwits a terrifying headmistress. However, Matilda is not a 'school story' per se, because the central theme is about attitudes to justice from the perspective of children. The literature genres most pertinent here are those that focus on the experience of school specifically – and particularly those that introduce us to themes related to testing and assessment in school settings.

During my research, I sought help from children's literature discussion forums, asking for lists of assessment-focused reading. The recommended reading revealed a dominant body of literature from the USA, but a growing collection from the UK too. The examples can be broadly categorised in two ways:

- stories focused on semi-realistic depictions of challenges in the lives of students, of which school experience, including assessment, is a key part of the narrative
- stories focused on assessment, specifically a high-stakes test or an examination that leads the overall narrative of the book.

Both categories are connected by what Gruner (2009) describes as the core 'business' of a young person's life: their experience of education in school. The success of the characters' time in school is most commonly symbolised as the qualifications achieved and the grades attained. The prevailing message across these types of children's literature is focused on the power of educational outcomes and the perpetuation of particular beliefs.

Work by the Nigerian academic Odejide (1987), who explores children's literature in African contexts, presents a close analysis of post-colonial narratives, where the theme of school achievement is popular. She identified key messages of competition and success at all costs: 'Competition is integral to this educational system; at the level of the individual, it is confined to academic performance and the desire for popularity among peers' (Odejide, 1987: 83). Some of the stories collected by Odejide also unashamedly promote a narrative in which boys must dominate, and the idea of a girl scoring higher than a boy is characterised as shameful.

Such ideas about educational success are problematic, as they establish unrealistic expectations and reflect a culture of social conditioning in school. This is explained well in the following:

> Education is centrally concerned with power; educational institutions regulate the ways in which children develop agency in the world. Thus, focusing on magical, already empowered children makes clear the importance of education as an institution of social control because in books such as the Harry Potter series, the protagonists learn when not to use their magic.
>
> (Gruner, 2009: 218)

The themes running through all of the above literatures include daily lessons, the pressures of homework and test preparation. These genres often present attitudes to academic work that are based on a reductive, narrow view of education. In Chapter 2, I reflected on how approaches to learning can be compromised and limited by assessment (Entwistle and Ramsden, 2015) and a yearning for good grades. Within such contexts, the purpose of learning is often confused with a rather intangible final outcome that hinges on getting it correct (no matter what 'it' is). For example, in Rowling's *Harry Potter* series (Rowling, 1997, 1998, 1999, 2000, 2004, 2006, 2007), both Harry Potter and Ron Weasley (his best friend) often ask Hermione Grainger (their academically able friend) to 'check' their homework. While the teachers among us know that working with others is a good revision tactic, Rowling characterises this behaviour in instrumentalist terms, with the protagonists focusing on simply getting the right answers.

At this point, you might be thinking: this is children's literature, it's escapist fiction about wizards and boarding schools, so why should I be concerned with whether or not the protagonists enjoy learning? My unease here concerns the continued subliminal messages that are conveyed through the texts that represent experiences readers can connect with because the school experience is assessment-focused. In *Harry Potter and the Prisoner of Azkaban* (Rowling, 1999), the focus on high-stakes testing is central to the story, with Hermione using a 'Time Turner' to literally travel through time in order to be able to study three times the number of subjects as her peers. The teachers at Hogwarts endorse such intensive revision and goals, but such an extreme itinerary means that she becomes increasingly tired, stressed and anxious as the story progresses.

The description of examination stress is very evocative: 'Exam week began and an unnatural hush fell over the castle. The third-years emerged from Transfiguration at lunchtime on Monday limp and ashen-faced, comparing results and bemoaning the difficulty of the tasks they had been set' (Rowling, 1999: 337). We can all sympathise with the students and acknowledge that sense of doom and dread. Rowling's decision to depict these issues simply illustrates their omnipresence in education.

Nevertheless, anxiety related to assessment, in particular to school examinations, is nothing new in children's literature. As an avid reader of Blyton's *Malory Towers* series as a child, I was fascinated by the emphasis placed on passing tests, the notion of 'cramming' and the deep disappointment felt by key characters who failed to do well despite the highly structured curriculum at boarding schools. In both the Malory Towers and St Clare's series (see, for example, Blyton, 1941, 1948), we encounter girls so desperate to get high grades in the School Certificate (the school-leaving examination of the time) that they resort to cheating. Such behaviour is always found out; the perpetrators are ostracised by their peers as a localised punishment, unless it can be proved that they are ill and so are forgiven, and afforded support and care until they are well again. Following such experiences, the wayward students fall into line and don't cheat again; in fact, they often become noted as being academically able in subsequent stories. Such tableaux of school life were fascinating to me as a child, as they contrasted strongly with my own experience.

Historically, school literature tends to feature the unique situation of boarding schools, but contemporary fiction takes a deeper dive into the testing experience in school situations that are more recognisable to readers. At the younger end of the children's literature spectrum, the popular Clarice Bean challenges the tests that she has to endure on a regular basis (and these reflect tests related to the Literacy and Numeracy strategies of the time). In *Clarice Bean Spells Trouble*, the character poses fundamental questions relating to the efficacy of test taking:

> Tuesday is not my favourite day because there is testing to see how clever everyone one is and how can you see that in a test? That's the thing about school, they might only test you for one thing i.e. Maths or spellingy type things or punctuationy thingummybobs. Maybe you know how to mend your hem with a stapler or stand on your actual head. But they do not test you for these things because the people who come up with the testing do not think this is important.
>
> (Child, 2004: 10)

Clarice's reflections on testing align with an eight-year-old girl's some-what unsophisticated perspective on the world, but they also reflect the frustration felt by many children about what testing is for and just why it is (or indeed is not) valuable.

In the USA, there are more texts that use testing as their central focus. For example, Poydar's (2005) *The Biggest Test in the Universe* fol-lows Sam and his class as they prepare for a standardised test. The book examines the fears that children spread between themselves and includes some of the common 'prompts' that are used to help children prepare. We find that the 'tips' provided by former test-takers actually make Sam feel more afraid! The tips are fairly broad ranging and include practical things (what to eat and bring) and behavioural recommendations (don't worry, get a good night's sleep, and practise techniques such as using flashcards – but the reader can see that one adviser says to use flashcards, while another cautions against this). So what is Sam to think? Such hints are, indeed, all potential ways to improve coping with stress, but they are also primers, reminding students of the fear generated by testing situ-ations in school settings. Poydar's book, like most in this genre, ends on a positive note. Sam takes the test and the world doesn't end, but he per-petuates the testing myth by telling his younger sister how terrifying it was – and so the cycle continues.

In *Testing Miss Malarkey* (Finchler and O'Malley, 2003), a class of primary-aged students tell the story of a school's preparation for a stand-ardised test called the Instructional Performance Through Understanding. The tables are turned in this book, as the students witness how the stress related to the upcoming test is impacting their teachers' behaviour and changing key aspects of the school culture. The popular Miss Malarkey publicly reveals the extent of her stress about testing, when the students notice she is biting her nails. Around the school, the general environment is changing too: the school principal keeps losing his temper, and medi-tation classes are introduced – and even the lunchtime menus change. The school lunches start to include lots of fish, reflecting the contentious claim that fish oils enhance neurological function (Abu-Ouf and Jan, 2014; Al-Ghannami et al., 2019), and parents are urged to attend a school meeting to discuss the meaning of the test results. While such stories are written with the intention of quelling test anxiety (Fiore, 2012), they also continue to top up the fear, by unintentionally adding to the burden of reminders about what tests mean.

Another US author, Julia Cook, has attempted to challenge the test-ing culture in American schools by creating a popular publication, *The Anti-Test Anxiety Society* (Cook et al., 2014). This resource is well used in US schools and fits with the models for counselling students in test preparation. The book includes cues and instructions for how to relax, what to eat, how to breathe, who to ask for help and so on. Bertha, our young female protagonist explains, much like Clarice Bean, how much she dislikes tests, because: 'To me, the word test stands for Terrible Every Single Time, because that's how I always do on them, TERRIBLE' (Cook *et al.*, 2014: 5). Bertha learns strategies to practise the tests, to stay calm, to exercise and eventually she becomes an expert test-taker in how she navigates practice papers, working strategically to maximise her opportunity to gain marks. Ultimately, she is able to amend her TEST acronym to Terrific Every Single Time by implementing a 12-step programme to challenge anxiety. A good thing? I'm not sure, but there is a website to go with the books, so why not take a look for yourself.

For the older readership, the theme of high-stakes testing set in dystopian futures is very popular both in books and on film. Two trilogies, *The Hunger Games* (Collins, 2011) and *The Testing* (Charbonneau, 2013), present societies that are situated in grim totalitarian regimes dominated by the highest of high-stakes testing: public competitions, where the prize is life itself. A very readable analysis of such fiction is offered by Alexander and Black (2015), who suggest that such narratives provide unique opportunities for us to explore the meaning and impact of testing on students' lives, because they present events that echo the lives of the readers.

A newly emerging genre in children's literature comes from China, where there is a fast-growing appetite for realist teenage fiction and, within this, a sub-genre of 'problem writing' (Li, 2017: 391). 'Problem writing' focuses on vulnerable children living in complex circumstances; within such contexts, the role of school, family and socio-economic constraints looms large. The exploration of realist authors in China is still very much an evolving culture. It treads a careful line between describing key issues that affect young people and making direct criticisms of the state. Chinese education policy of the past two decades has been characterised in *Quality Education in China EQO (Essential-qualities-oriented) Education* (Xie, 2002), which focuses on education for so-called twenty-first-century skills. Despite the promotion of skills such as creativity, innovation and problem-solving, the problem fiction depicts school life as being dominated by testing and anxiety generated by labelling students as either weak or successful based on exam results (for example, Louie and Louie, 2002).

It seems to me that we need to ask: Why are students getting this stressed? And, more importantly, why are we making them this stressed?

Perhaps it is time to recognise that even the writing and publication of books that fictionalise concerns about high-stakes tests reveal a narrow conception of achievement. The extent of the portrayal of assessment in more popular forms of print media is unclear, as it takes time to amass examples, but it is there – and it presents educational assessment in both positive and negative ways. One place where it does appear continually, and where it is criticised, loved, debated and hated, is on social media. The next section discusses a selection of the current issues in this very particular environment.

(Anti-)social media

Social media is an integral part of the lives of young people, especially school students the world over; almost 90 per cent of 16–24-year-olds now regularly use at least one form of social media (Eurostat, 2019). The statistics on social media use are constantly shifting and new users appear daily, while others undergo digital detoxes to extricate themselves from the pressures of a life lived online. Comprehensive quarterly summaries of global data relating to digital communications are published on the We Are Social website (We Are Social UK and Hootsuite, 2021). The April 2021 publication reports that internet use, internet access, mobile phone use and social media interactions continue to grow, with more than 60 per cent of the world's population now online. There are some inequitable trends that persist: for example, women are still less likely to have internet access compared to men; and broad public access is still confined to the wealthiest nations globally.

Social media dominates online interactions, with recent data (Newman, 2021) revealing that, globally, approximately 17 new users join a social media platform every second! The important difference of social media compared to other forms of communication is that its longevity depends on user-generated content. It needs 'feeding' because, as explained by van Dijck (2013) in *The Culture of Connectivity*, the genesis of social media is based on the human need to connect and to communicate.

The COVID-19 pandemic has made this even more obvious, and has influenced the use of social media in many countries as populations had to change their modes of communication due to lockdowns. There are three global giants in the social media world: WhatsApp is favourite, with almost one quarter (24.1 per cent) of 16–64-year-olds using it regularly; just behind follows Facebook (21.8 per cent); and then comes Instagram (18.4 per cent).

It is important to remember that school-aged students, those most affected by assessment, are least likely to share their discussions on WhatsApp or Facebook, because these are not the place for those kinds of communications. The way that social media has played a role in high-stakes testing has become a part of the global online assessment discourses, but it seems that these conversations unfold in particular settings and in particular ways. Students who feel a need to talk about testing will do so where they know that those who have a stake in the tests – namely their teachers, the exam boards, university admissions staff – might be reading.

What social media has done for young people is to create a new culture, where they share a great deal of personal information in very public spaces. This prolific exchange of text, images and video is now encapsulated in the phrase 'oversharing', which became a recognised part of our language in 2016 (Chandler and Munday, 2016). This idea of talking about all aspects of our lives in public spaces is relatively uncharted territory, so we can't be sure how damaging or not such behaviours might be in the long term. Contemporary research about the danger of social media use is mixed (Buglass *et al.*, 2016), with some studies demonstrating positive aspects, such as enhanced self-esteem and enriched social communications. However, other research blames it for a range of social ills – from the prevalence of cyberbullying to a more general undermining of good mental health.

While much of the concern about the darker side of social networking is often sensationalised in news media, we should be wary of its accuracy. However, research (for example, Braun and Gillespie, 2011; Roberts and David, 2019; Newman *et al.*, 2020) is revealing specific issues that seem to affect young people in their use of social media, and some of these are useful to consider when looking at how assessment discourses unfold in online spaces. For example, when students use social media as a means of 'broadcasting' their feelings, comments and responses, they become the reporter; they take on this role with a sense of self-determination. Social media sites were originally designed as a way of creating a 'club' – a place to share and communicate with others. Originating in universities, their remit has adapted, and now students use them as a place to seek solace. They also provide a platform where a particularised reflection of achievements can be presented. For example, students can post pictures of themselves in favourable poses, filtered to perfection, or they might post commentaries on the slog of revision or their fear about exams.

Over the course of five years, I have watched social networking during high-stakes testing cycles and noted that particular themes tend to dominate at different times in the cycle. While most of my interactions and viewing tend to be in the UK, the issues I see are by no means geographically specific. Indeed, the fast-paced development of social media use reveals patterns of discourse common to students (and often their teachers) across the globe. As Bourke (2019) argues, it is important to 'listen' to the dialogue in these spaces, to better understand the lived experience of students. It is equally important to note that, of course, those who comment on social media are not representative of the entire student population engaging in test taking, but there are some notable trends that seem to gather momentum during a testing cycle and which seem to relate to yet more duality: expectations and end results.

Expectations

The lead-up to actually taking examinations means dealing with stress, and a common way to do this is by using self-deprecation as a protective mechanism. Social media actually provides a really engaging space in which to express fears and anxieties (Sutch and Klir, 2017), and the popularity of memes – visual messages that are widely shared on the internet – often brings some comedy to a challenging situation. From 2019 to 2021, a popular theme in England was clowns. On both Twitter and Instagram feeds, students expressed concern about their experiences by posting pictures of clowns, sometimes actually making themselves up as clowns and adding commentary. The commentaries vary from the positive (a student is pleased with the questions they can answer) to the all-or-nothing discourses common to social media (a student is despairing at revising a broad range of content, only to have a few topics appear on the paper).

While both of these scenarios are relatively positive, there also follow many postings that represent assessment dysmorphic behaviours, portraying the exam experience as catastrophic and predicting failure. There is safety in expecting the worst; indeed, psychological studies examining performance anxiety (for example, Eysenck, 1979; Zhang et al., 2018) suggest that deflecting any blame for potential failure is common when individuals feel under duress. Therefore, it is usual to see postings by students on social media that apportion blame at the start of the exam experience, usually directed at the exam boards and sometimes the teachers, in order to prepare for an uncertain future.

This is still very much an evolving area in education, but what is notable is that across the assessment industry, careful attention is being paid to social media. Strategists are now employed to watch social media feeds and consider how best to respond when issues beset key examination processes. One of the few reports on this in the UK is from Cambridge Assessment: Sutch and Klir (2017) found peaks and troughs of inter-action, with most posts happening the night before an exam and then late on the actual day when a high-stakes exam was being taken. This is per-haps unsurprising, as students will be likely to share ideas, fears and so on in preparation, and then return to social media as a release once the exam is over. Sutch and Klir's findings suggest that the tone and words used change according to the context and timing – and this is something that could be of further interest. Words such as 'luck' and 'hope' appeared commonly in the lead-up to the exams. This reflects those memes I men-tioned earlier, which often signal luck as being imperative. Once the test-ing cycle is over, the focus moves to difficulty. Sutch and Klir (2017) also found students becoming less hopeful about the outcomes, reflected in the types of emoji used – more tearful, afraid, unhappy – linked to tweets.

While sharing concerns is a common response to a stress-filled situ-ation such as high-stakes testing, it is the wide and fast-spreading activity of sharing that makes for different discourses in contemporary educa-tional settings. The priming effects mentioned in Chapter 2 are worth recalling here – it is hard to evidence just yet, but do the quick-fire post-ings and responses engender fear, confidence, anxiety and more? I pro-pose that perhaps these heightened discussions of expected failure and fear feed some disproportionately negative responses to the end results.

We are all perhaps accustomed to seeing images of national exam results day; it is a globally recognisable experience across all phases of education, but especially when the stakes are high. In terms of social media postings, just entering a search term such as #examresults (and the year date, such as 2021) will result in feeds peppered with postings of joy, misery and everything in between. The few days prior to results publication reveal a growing concern, as the following examples from Twitter demonstrate. One tweet signals fear that life will be over after results day, in other words they have three days left: '3 days to live my best life #Resultsday2019'. Another confidently predicts no sleep the night before results publication: 'Why not have a twitter sleepover since a lot of people won't be sleeping Wednesday night? #Resultsday2019 #GCSEs2019'.

Colleges and schools promote and actively market the achievement of their students using social media. This way of communicating success (because failure or mediocrity go unmentioned) is another reflection of publicly signalling an educational establishment's place and power. It discloses the competition between establishments and, through the use of social media, is a well-targeted means of advertising the success of students during the annual furore that surrounds exam results. Positive posts to urge engagement appear first: '#Goodluck to all our amazing students this morning collecting their #GCSEresults! We'll be waiting in the Hall from 9am – see you there!' Then, on the big day, the tone changes to ramp up the excitement and focus on the highest fliers. We see posts that include messages of success, extraordinary feats and lots of students literally jumping for joy. These images underpin the need for public demonstrations of success; they are in danger of demoralising those who cannot, perhaps ever, hit top marks.

While I accept that there is nothing wrong in presenting success and the positive outcomes for schools and their students, this is not representative of the majority of students. Interviews with education journalists in the UK made me reconsider the value of these kinds of reporting because, as one interviewee said, 'the role of the journalist is to create a story, and one that will sell'. There is no market in journalists writing about or photographing the 'also-ran' candidates, because there is nothing sensational in their normality. What social media brings to the discourse surrounding results are voices that appeal and challenge.

A recent and popular phenomenon has been for students to record themselves opening their exam results live on YouTube. This is a risky event, because of course when things don't unfold as expected, there is nowhere to hide. I should note that it is also important to be cautious about the validity of these recordings – for example, it is clear that students curate these postings. However, in terms of considering the discourses circling in shared public spaces (the YouTube videos on results day usually have approximately 4,000 views – rising to tens of thousands for students who are influencers). These postings indicate some signs of assessment dysmorphia, and examples of misaligned expectations are revealed. In 2019, Lily (not her real name), a student from a sixth-form college in the east of England, posted the following:

> I can understand like its okay whatever I get, I messed up. I'm going to go into college and check the marks I got in those papers for English and I'm going to ask for a remark for the sake of my dignity, not for uni!

Lily achieved a B for English and an A and a C for her other subjects. While these were not the grades necessary to meet her university offers, they are by no means indicative of failure or even of 'messing up'. What interested me in Lily's response was the need to seek dignity via a remark. This also suggests that she does not believe in the efficacy of the result or that she could have scored less than an A.

While I ponder the curious nature of how students perceive their educational achievements, such evidence suggests how closely results are intertwined with the individual's sense of academic self.

'She's a perfect 9'

The pressure to be a perfect 9 (the highest grade at GCSE level in England) is highlighted in the dialogues which are patrolled by disembodied voices warning young people that not only do they have to look a certain way, but they must also achieve only the highest marks – or they are a failure. Setting unattainable goals has a myriad of influences and potential outcomes.

In *The Case Against Perfection*, Sandel (2007) considers the influence of genetic engineering and how it has led to a quest to perfect ourselves. Sandel's analysis includes discussion of how elite athletes can engineer their performance, using performance-enhancing technologies that don't break the rules of the game, but are questionable in terms of how we conceptualise sport versus a spectacle. What this means in educational terms is whether we value the aim of education itself, as a concept, rather than simply viewing its value purely in terms of test results. When I discussed the idea of assessment dysmorphic behaviour in Chapter 4, I was proposing that we want to encourage students to be the very best they can, but that the craving for high attainment should never be at the expense of healthy – or even ethical – behaviour.

The difficulty here is in balancing reality with the dream. In contemporary educational establishments, it is common to hear mantras pressing students to aim higher and to reach for the stars, praising those (few) who make the grade. Through popular literatures (in print and online) the messages of difficulty and competitiveness act as reminders and reinforcement to see assessment as something that is a battle – and even something sinister. Finally, in the newest settings for global communication – social media – we see students taking charge of many areas of what they consider their spaces, to explore, to explain and sometimes to explode with the effort directed at educational assessments.

All of these messages circulating in public settings constantly provide a conflicting series of challenges and ideas about how we are to view educational assessment and its value. What concerns me most about some of the discourses is how they subtly reinforce that dichotomy of success or failure in the context of assessment *and* how they frame education in a test-focused way. The final two chapters attempt to reorientate discourses of assessment and to challenge those blinkered, reductive views of educational achievement.

6
Introducing assessment literacy

Chapters 1 to 5 presented the issues that are currently impacting assessment policy and practice, and how they are perceived by key users and stakeholders across education and within the assessment industry. These issues are complex and difficult challenges to address but, as I have argued, we need to do just that.

Chapters 6 and 7 are shorter and together provide ideas for recommendations of how to reframe the discourses circling assessment, in order to improve and promote confidence. Such changes have the potential to provide a foundation for more accessible explanations of assessment practice, and to feed them back into the wider education discourses, with the aim of breaking the binary arguments and allowing space for a range of views.

The theme of binary thinking and attitudes is central to all of the discourses discussed and to how we can grasp a better understanding of educational assessment. In this chapter, I argue that a clear understanding of assessment literacy is vital as the public discourses which focus on education broaden to include an ever-widening range of media outlets. An explanation of the current view of assessment literacy provides the starting point here. Given that it generally focuses on improving the assessment literacy of teachers, I intend to argue the case for better explanations and presentation of evidence, so that a wide public assessment audience can improve their assessment literacy too. Creating good assessment (Gipps, 2012) is not enough without engagement and understanding; it is important that we create a sense of valuing the role of assessment that moves beyond a grade or mark.

A significant problem with becoming literate about assessment is the challenge required by reflecting on practice and changing our view in accordance with new evidence. It's a difficult thing to do, and was well summarised by John Dewey (1910: 13):

> Reflective thinking is always more or less troublesome because it involves overcoming the inertia that inclines one to accept suggestions at their face value; it involves willingness to endure a condition of mental unrest and disturbance. Reflective thinking, in short, means judgment suspended during further inquiry; and suspense is likely to be somewhat painful.

I consider here the various means by which we can – or should – improve assessment literacy: from teacher education (both in university postgraduate courses and in school-based training provision), through understanding and appreciating the variety of assessments and how they provide discrete value to student learning and, more broadly, through ways to promote better public literacy discourses through the media explored in earlier chapters.

What does assessment literacy mean?

Understanding the importance of assessment practice means being aware that it is not a fixed entity. It is a crucial part of teaching practice, and when policymakers, parents, students or teachers attempt to divide assessment and teaching/learning, this immediately reduces the potential quality of any learning experience. Any discourse that claims the two must be viewed separately fails to understand the role of the teacher, and how they are continually assessing and concerned with assessment-related activities in their professional role. This merging of the two activities is hypothesised in academic settings as 'assessment literacy' or simply 'being assessment-literate'.

The idea of assessment literacy was first written about by Rick Stiggins (1991, 1993, 1995, 2014) in the USA. Stiggins was concerned about what he termed a 'devotion' to test outcomes as the driver for education policy, when there is little information in a discrete grade that can actually tell us how well an education system is performing. Given the dominance of education testing in the USA, his claims are contentious; his continued championing of how to educate and improve assessment literacy is important in how we consider ways of improving public confidence in assessment more broadly.

The meaning of assessment literacy is difficult to unpack, primarily because it comprises a range of interacting variables, many of which are difficult to control. Put simply, assessment literacy is the ability to understand assessment, and then use it appropriately within the educational context in which you are working. While this seems straightforward, in reality it is not, because assessment practice is imperfect. What really matters, argued Stiggins (1995: 253), is a teacher's awareness of the 'alarms' – those warnings that are stimulated by errors and problems that arise in any assessment process.

However, this is where it becomes more complex, because acknowledging the alarm is not enough. To enact literacy means having the agency to actually make effective changes. To a casual observer, it might appear straightforward to make such changes, but the reality is very different. The power and agency to make changes is not always within the grasp of teachers (in any phase of education), because:

> When teachers assess, more is in play than simply knowledge and skills. They may have knowledge of what is deemed effective practice, but not be confident in their enactment of such practice. They may have knowledge, and have confidence, but not believe that assessment processes are effective. Most importantly, based on their prior experiences and their context, they may consider that some assessment processes should not be a part of their role as teachers and in interactions with students. Teachers can, quite literally, have mixed feelings about assessment.
>
> (Looney *et al.*, 2017: 455)

There is research and there are resources to facilitate the assessment literacy of teachers in schools, but there is still a broader context to consider. The changing public discourses around education – and, particularly, those focused on assessment – reveal a need for access to resources that will also facilitate public literacy of the topic.

What can we expect of assessment literacy?

While I want to consider the idea of assessment literacy in a broad context, this section focuses initially on formal education settings – schools and colleges – simply because this is where we most commonly engage in high-stakes testing and assessments. My proposition is that we should introduce assessment literacy as a part of our education systems, to embed the notion that assessment is not something that happens *after* learning.

The work of Dann (2002, 2014, 2018) is valuable here. Her research in primary schools demonstrates how assessments are conceptualised and then how understanding can be reoriented, so that the value of different assessments, and those that help to develop learning in particular, becomes appreciated. Dann (2002: 142) proposed the notion of assessment *as* learning:

> There is little account taken of the ways in which assessment processes (rather than outcomes) influence learning processes. Those that do exist tend to highlight adverse stress-related pressures linked to summative tests—usually through the popular press. Although the concerns raised should have an important place in our research and thinking they should not be at the expense of other strands of inquiry which endeavour to look beneath the surface of experiences dominated by national summative assessment systems.

A serious consideration of promoting assessment literacy should include how students and their teachers understand their summative and formative experiences. Building on Dann's quote above, our obsession with assessment remains focused largely on test outcomes within the confines of a measurement-dominated characterisation of what constitutes success in education. Howell (2013: 9) provides a compelling argument for the value of assessment literacy as being 'an extremely important teaching function that contributes to many other aspects of teaching, such as instruction and classroom management', because these functions are indicators of quality in educational experience.

The practice of determining the outcomes of high-stakes national tests – the process of awarding – is not well understood. This should not be a surprise, because it happens externally from school. However, it is time that this was better understood and generally demystified. Understanding assessment processes linked to high-stakes qualifications is actually a focus of both students and teachers in the years leading up to final examinations, when the learning and teaching is constrained by a syllabus or by specifications set by the attendant awarding body. It is common, particularly in those discourses of doom mentioned in Chapter 5, to see claims that examination boards, regulatory bodies and/or government departments are devising cunning plans to abuse students and schools. Such discourses are unhelpful, because they are lazy in their simplicity and do not acknowledge the complexity of assessment practice.

According to Popham (2017), there are two motivations to support assessment literacy: being sure to use the right assessment for 'the job', so that the outcomes are useful and a truthful characterisation of student performance; and accepting the fact that powerful assessment happens in classroom settings too – teachers are to be trusted in this matter. These motivations are linked to an earlier mention of standards in education (see Chapters 1 and 2), and how our perception of standards shapes our beliefs about learning and assessment.

Being literate in assessment has the potential to challenge key concerns about the reliability of assessment outcomes, so ensuring that we know what we mean when we talk about standards is central to any discussion about literacy too. This is no easy task, particularly given that even the most recent detailed studies of international standards (see Baird *et al.*, 2018) reveal the extent to which standards are characterised by a particular assessment ethos, and most importantly, by 'cultural and contextual conditions within the country' (Isaacs and Gorgen, 2018: 308).

In short, assessment literacy matters because there are ethical imperatives tied to how all stakeholders use and interpret assessment. This might appear to be an overblown proposition, but using appropriate assessments that fit the student, the task and the situation matters, because it improves the educational experience for both learner and teacher. The integrity necessary to support such a goal can only be achieved by committing to assessment literacy.

Introducing assessment literacy in school-level and national discourses will not only improve broader public understanding, but can also prepare students better for further education, because as research in tertiary settings has found, the discourses of duality still reign supreme. Taken as a whole, assessment practices in higher education are typically characterised by the dominant discourse of the testing cultures that are focused on the measurement of knowledge using largely summative assessments to designate the award of a degree. Yet Rust (2007: 233) describes many of these summative marking practices as not only unfair but 'intellectually and morally indefensible, and statistically invalid'. Rust's argument here relates to the claims of precision in marking, including acceptance that markers might be able to distinguish a standard, particularly in humanities subjects, that can be graded to one precise percentage point. He claims that the validity of grade awarding in higher education institutions is negatively impacted by 'idiosyncratic institutional rules' (Rust: 2007: 233–4). He has a valid point – it's all about assessment literacy.

The majority of assessment evidence (that is, coursework and examinations) used for school-based high-stakes tests is set, marked and awarded by agencies external to the schools and colleges themselves. However, within universities the majority of assessment is set, marked and awarded by academics, and specific education in assessment is not required as a part of their role. This contrasts strongly with the highly skilled test developers and examiners used by examination boards; they have to be subject experts and are required to follow professional development training to ensure that they work to a high level (for details in England, see Joint Council for Qualifications, 2021b). Marking for high-stakes tests such as GCSEs and A levels is subject to detailed scrutiny within marking teams, so that if one individual's marking is erratic, a senior marker will step in and that batch will be marked again to ensure that the standard is met (see Joint Council for Qualifications, 2021b, for a more detailed account of this process). Simply put – the individuals involved in test development at exam boards, the markers of high-stakes national tests and the subject-expert awarding teams are all highly skilled assessors, who have very high levels of assessment literacy.

Of course, they are not perfect, and neither is the system – there will always be errors (Koretz, 2008; Popham, 2017), largely because assessment systems are designed and managed by human beings. There are also statistical errors which occur within testing regimes too – not those incorrectly titled 'mutant algorithms' that the English prime minister alleged had hurt students in the summer of 2020; rather, these are what statisticians call a standard error, which is part of any large data set. Including better understanding of issues such as the meaning and occurrence of error should be integral to any curriculum for assessment literacy, because attention paid to this could challenge the fake news and falsehoods that cling to national tests and testing systems.

In higher education, there is work to do in terms of developing assessment literacy for all members of the so-called academy: staff and students. This is because the systems remain internal to each institution, and this is largely true of undergraduate and postgraduate education globally (OECD, 2010, 2018). While national standards for teaching, learning and assessment are set in most countries and jurisdictions (Amaral and Rosa, 2014), there remains some ambiguity in relation to what Bloxham and Price (2016) suggest is unchallenged understanding and assumptions about what constitutes the relevant standard at an institution.

The increase in grade outcomes across the higher education sector (see Chapter 3) should be of concern, because it might be that a poor level of assessment literacy is undermining the classification system within universities. Even at undergraduate level, where individuals are making an active choice to go to university, the general attitudes to learning remain limited and often superficial – those discourses of doom and desire still dominate. Students have a desire to hold an undergraduate degree or even a higher degree, but as Boud *et al.* (2010) argue, students have difficulty in shifting their focus beyond measurements (that is, grades) as evidence of successful assessment practice.

Therefore, it is unsurprising that students remain focused on ways that will enhance their chances of passing, rather than on learning for its own sake. Two decades ago, the Australian academic David Boud (2000: 151) introduced the term 'double duty'. He claimed that despite assessments being designed with one aim, their function rarely remains so, because it is all too easy for schools, teachers and the students themselves to expect assessments to multi-task. Boud suggested that in universities, assessments are used to simultaneously provide feedback that helps students develop as learners and summative certification; to focus on something immediate in terms of learning, but with one eye on equipping students for an often unknown future career.

The complexity of managing assessment practice in higher education is pausing the evolution of assessment literacy in universities. As research from Australia (Boud and Soler, 2016; Bearman *et al.*, 2017), Hong Kong (Carless, 2020), Canada (Volante and Fazio, 2007) and the UK (Medland, 2014, 2015, 2016, 2019) reveals, the preoccupation is with *certification of mastery* rather than *actual mastery* of a subject or skills. This skewed approach leads to a continued cycle of what can only be described as poor assessment practice; it has to change. I don't wish to apportion blame here; rather, what needs to happen is a commitment to creating literate assessors, literate students (those being assessed) and literate assessment bystanders (see Figure 6.1), who may or may not have a defined stake in the process.

Becoming a literate assessor

High-quality assessment is aligned with similarly high levels of assessment literacy (Stiggins, 1995; Black and Wiliam, 2018). It would seem logical to surmise, therefore, that assessment literacy is a necessary condition for high-quality teaching. This follows the argument that assessment is an integral part of teaching and learning, as opposed to something that happens once the learning is deemed complete. A commitment to assessment literacy that seeks to improve both how we assess and how we build confidence in this element of education has to start from the agreed assumption that assessment is integral to pedagogy. So what does a literate assessor look like?

There are some emerging themes that can help to offer a model for starting and maintaining assessment literacy, but I don't believe that there is one single way to do this. In many senses, it mirrors the complexity of assessment itself. The one thing it requires of teachers, and of those entrenched in the accepted norms of our assessment cultures, is a willingness to change.

An example from Marilyn Fleer (2015) articulates how assessors have to begin by engaging in a process of reconstructing their beliefs and understanding about assessment and assessment theory. Fleer (2015: 227) argues that this education for literacy requires teachers to reflect carefully on their own attitudes and habits, and also to research what she terms 'assessment interactions' with students. These can be collated and I present them in Figure 6.1.

What this reveals is the challenge that assessors are not only watched and judged by a range of stakeholders, but also have to

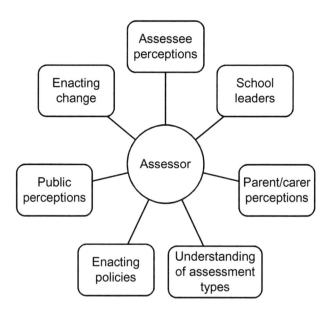

Figure 6.1 Assessment interactions: how to become a literate assessor.
Source: Author

consistently 'upskill' and learn to be able to adapt to new policies, to try new pedagogies and to accept constant change. Assessors need to reconcile individual and collective activities, while understanding the pressures, policy and sociocultural contexts within which all of this is happening. The broader issues have to be a part of any literacy education, because they impact on how assessors improve their understanding and use of assessments in education.

Research consistently indicates that literacy relating to formative assessment methods can have positive effects on student achievement (Black and Wiliam, 1998; Wiliam, 2009, 2017; Black, 2013). Several decades of research, particularly in the UK, New Zealand and Australia (for example, Wiliam, 2001; OECD, 2005; Hattie, 2007; Hattie and Brown, 2010; Van Der Kleij et al., 2018) have found that using formative assessment techniques is successful, because they allow both teachers and students to refocus on teaching and evaluation of understanding, as opposed to memorisation and recall strategies that dominate examinations and other forms of summative assessment. While advocates of formative assessment practices will champion the regular use of a range of assessment types, they would also argue that it is a continued education for users of assessment strategies that will make them useful and relevant as ways to support and summarise learning. Investment in professional development and ensuring that its value is duly noted are paramount, if a foundation for assessment literacy is to be created. This applies not only in England, but globally too.

Acknowledging the tensions relating to assessment choice, and decision-making for assessors generally, is a significant responsibility. Looking forward, assessors need to learn ways to communicate better with those outside educational establishments. Fleer (2015) suggests that we are still a long way off breaking down the barriers between home and school in this regard. I would say that the fallout from COVID-19 and the experiences of homeschooling may have provided many families (and others) with a different view of what really happens in schools. However, it should not be taken as read that those who aren't assessors will be keen to learn, and I would not propose that it becomes the sole responsibility of assessors to make this work.

Broadening assessment literacy

Acceptance of something as important as a testing system might be desirable, but it is no substitute for understanding what that is and its implications for the individual who is being assessed and/or other stake-holders. I would not expect full-scale acceptance of assessment processes and practice, but my goal here is to suggest that we look to developing an informed understanding, one that can challenge those broad, ill-informed binary views that haunt public discourses on assessment. Countering the misinformation little by little is the way forward, similar to those marginal gains (Hall *et al.*, 2012) that saw the British cycling team dominate the world in track cycling.

Any commitment to change involves those who are being assessed, usually students, because they know what it is to be assessed and they might have a good understanding of national testing systems, but that is not the same as being assessment literate. The heart of my argument is to create discourses underpinned by realism that will better support not only students but also those who feel they have a stake in the assessment processes in education. Being realistic, we might not always hear things that we like, for example: you have failed that test. But such discourses can also include statements to invoke hope and curiosity to change our perceptions of assessment.

As always, such discourses are helped with philosophical thinking. Try not to imagine that an approach to literacy is one-directional; rather, it is more helpful to understand that it is okay to be more-or-less realistic about the particular nature of assessment literacy. Stiggins (2014: 71) presents an enticing (and perhaps tongue-in-cheek) 'Bill of Rights' for students being assessed:

- Students are entitled to know the purpose for each assessment in which they participate; that is, they have a right to know specifically how the results will be used and by whom.
- Students are entitled to know and understand the learning targets reflected in the exercises and scoring guide that make up any and all assessments.
- Students are entitled to understand the differences between good and poor performance on pending assessments and to learn to self-assess their progress towards self-mastery.
- Students are entitled to dependable assessment of their achievement, gathered using high-quality assessments.
- Students are entitled to effective communication of their assessment results, whether those results are being delivered to them, their families or others concerned with their academic well-being.

The instrumental nature of this 'Bill of Rights' focuses mainly on the outcomes and, as such, could be misused in terms of becoming another inevitable tick list of targets. But Stiggins' idea here is interesting, because it gives students some ownership of the processes and practice at a fundamental level. It puts a stop to that prevailing idea that assessment is something we 'do' to students. However, Stiggins goes on to argue convincingly for the development of a community of practice involving the student, their parents/families and the assessors who work collectively to develop shared understanding of assessment and how it is conducted in society. Broadly speaking, this characterises what is necessary, if we are to improve public confidence and to challenge the binary discourses.

What is particularly useful in Stiggins' 'Bill of Rights' is that it opens up the core tensions in assessment: that students don't always like the tests they have to take, but it doesn't mean that they are not good tests. Ensuring that everyone understands the difference between the intrinsic validity of the assessment itself and the personal preference of the test-taker is at the heart of this debate. One of the most troubling aspects of the discourses evidenced in Chapter 5 is the misinformation and the misunderstandings that circulate freely on social media and in other public settings. The problem is that there is no space or time to reply and, perhaps more importantly, there is often little appetite for, or interest in, knowing what is correct – or indeed true.

As discussed in Chapters 3 and 4, it is important to acknowledge the complex nature of the wide-ranging discourses that surround students, teachers, parents and the wider public, and how these discourses influence perceptions of schools and education. One way we might challenge the existing discourses of assessment as testing and those grades that mark out a school as being good or not so good is to represent schools as places with a variety of missions, whose success is not underpinned by test outcomes alone. The current ethos of many schools includes laudable aims, such as developing good citizens, preparing students for the twenty-first century, building resilience and so on. However, our assessment systems currently tell students that they will be sorted, ranked and ready for allocation on completion of their education – all within the limited framework of national testing systems. It is time to change how this process works, otherwise we are at risk of returning to the assessment systems created alongside the Industrial Revolution (Curtis and Boultwood, 1962), with a production line of qualifications and certification solely for economic gain. Students deserve more than just being sorted along a continuum of achievement in education. As Stiggins

(2014: 69) says: 'important new missions [aims] have been added, and our assessment practices must accommodate them'.

Building new approaches to literacy is central to such an aim. As a lifelong distance runner, I stand by the claim that a longer-term understanding of the role and work of assessors is best conceived of as a marathon, never a sprint. Imagining that we can change educational thinking and policy quickly and successfully is neither helpful nor realistic. However, building a plan to enact change, to experiment, to invoke curiosity and provide opportunities for any and all stakeholders to share information, ideas and research about what works? That is surely worth investment.

7
A new road map for assessment?

In relation to some types of assessment, expectations are indeed great. It is difficult to shift the notion that a grade or a mark is the best reflection of ability, skill or knowledge, and despite the best efforts of researchers in education to offer opportunities and evidence of alternatives, change is slow to come. The idea that a single, simple measure can characterise the complex nature of learning is confounding, but also understandable. However, just as images of perfection in beauty advertising are now being challenged as unreal (Kleemans *et al.*, 2018; Huang *et al.*, 2021), and performers are asking that images of themselves are not artificially made sleek, slim and impossibly shiny, isn't it time to challenge the continual expectations of achievement in educational settings as being unrealistic? This final chapter draws together the key issues identified earlier, and presents ideas for improving how we can better understand – and then build confidence, and even trust, in – assessment practice.

I propose a new discourse of *assessment esteem*: that is, providing assurance that different types of assessment are useful when used appropriately, and that all have merit, even if, to paraphrase Lewis Carroll (2015), all those who take part don't have prizes. I propose the following:

- *discourses of confidence*: engendering confidence in assessment systems both within and beyond formal educational settings
- *discourses for reshaping*: creating evidence-based understanding of assessment to support change in policy and practice.

Discourses of confidence in assessment

To build confidence and engender trust, it is vital to decide where we might channel efforts for a movement towards improving assessment literacy, to create new discourses about assessment and its value. This cannot be the sole responsibility of one group or individual. As is often claimed (Stobart, 2008), assessment is a social activity and, as such, it requires a social perspective to facilitate its reform. Changes that have happened over many decades in many countries are generally what I consider to be akin to rearranging the deckchairs on the *Titanic* – it's time to move beyond mere tinkering.

Starting within educational establishments makes sense. As Michael Apple (2009: 41) elegantly argues, students (and, I would argue, their teachers too) are a captive audience to particular doctrines in education because 'Schools are key mechanisms for determining what is social valued as legitimate knowledge and what is seen as merely popular'. The public trust that surrounds schools is an important lever for change (and therein lie ways to break and rebuild some of those discourses outlined in Figure 1.2). The same issues arise beyond the school gates and within universities. It is time to change discourses about assessment and to help students come to terms with a range of ways to evidence their learning.

In all phases of education we face a significant challenge: defining what is the purpose of education. Creating a discourse of confidence in assessment means addressing three key aims:

- It is time for a new narrative of success in schools/colleges, so that students stop believing that their worth is based on a tiny number of examination results awarded at 16 or 18 years old.
- It is time to educate teachers in how to assess confidently and competently – to professionally upskill them in this regard, so that there is confidence in their role as equals in assessment alongside standardised, external testing.
- In universities, it is time to challenge the narrative that payment for study at degree level guarantees the award of that degree.

These aims present a range of challenges, because they are complex and require the capacity for change in attitudes to what are the social and cultural norms characterising success in education. I don't believe that this should prevent us from trying to see things differently, but it requires collective engagement to make it happen. Let's start by changing the narrative in schools.

Policymakers need to work with teacher education departments to re-evaluate the perception of teachers and for teachers to see just how important assessment is within their professional role. By this, I don't mean that they have to be taught how to write exam papers and run assessments at levels equivalent to those undertaken by the exam boards, but teachers do need to feel confident and competent to make judgements about their students that are not driven largely by accountability measures. Assessment theory and practice makes up a tiny slice of the packed curriculum guiding teacher education, yet in the reality of teachers' working lives, it consumes weeks and months of time (as Joe told us in Chapter 2). Scant attention is paid to the value and importance of assessment early in the professional life of teachers, and this supports a discourse that allows the sense of distance and a lack of confidence in being an assessor to flourish.

Once educated, qualified and working in schools, teachers need to be guaranteed continual professional development (which should include assessment). The discourse around this should be honest and transparent. That is, you don't just study a degree to teach and then do it. Being a teacher (in any phase of education) requires continual education, because learning and teaching don't stand still. Our understanding of learning is constantly evolving, our understanding of how we teach is constantly evolving, and the effectiveness of how we assess teaching and learning changes too. To imagine that this is something we now 'know' and is a fixed idea is both naive and dangerous. Such thinking underpins that discourse of duality, where types of assessment are set up as opponents and labelled as good or bad – worth something or valueless. Uncoupling the value of assessment from summative, high-stakes tests is key to breaking the discourses of duality. As I argued in Chapter 6, ensuring that we have literate assessors means that we have teachers with confidence and competence to do their job well. This good practice provides assurance in wider society beyond the school gates that all assessments, not just high-stakes tests, matter.

The discourse of assessment literacy – and respect for its existence – should also be central to those who are responsible for teaching and learning in educational settings beyond school. Assessment literacy is needed urgently in higher education because, as Norton *et al.* (2019) argue, academics receive almost no education on how to set, mark and moderate assessments. I don't mean to suggest that all assessment that happens in universities is faulty and open to dispute but, based on my claim above that education does not stand still, university staff need to be open to reflecting on and improving their work as assessors. The reality is that the kinds of experience and knowledge that are used to determine qualifications taken at school are far more rigorous than those determined by academics, and some of the research challenges the idea that the efficacy of standards in universities is comparable with that in schools.

The proposition of a discourse for esteemed assessment requires honesty on several counts:

- explaining what the limitations of assessment are: for example, that there is no perfect test or assessment of any kind and that error exists
- at a personal level, accepting that we can't all be good at everything: despite the variability in human competences and intellectual capacity, such things are rarely absolute and fixed
- learning to live with uncertainty, which will provide assessment esteem and also reduce the levels of stress that accompany our current belief systems related to high-stakes testing
- reorientating how we view assessment: from a measure to a means of developing personal skills of reflection and understanding, so equipping us to be more competent when facing change.

Creating a curriculum for assessment and confidence is something that could be realised for schools, but introducing this to a wider audience, for example in universities, is more of a challenge. This is where the reshaping really happens.

Discourses for reshaping assessment

As explained in Chapters 1–5, we take, create and represent discourses from a wide range of sources. So is it realistic to try to tackle all of these, in a quest to change how we talk about assessment? Not in all cases.

News

Understanding how news discourses are accessed and trusted is important to the central theme of this book, because news reporting stimulates public education debates. News websites and newspapers remain the primary source of public information globally for around 60 per cent of the world's population (Newman, 2021). However, what is evident is that different newspapers and news media outlets are, of course, aligned to particular ways of looking at education, so will present a range of ideas.

A solution here is to provide education for journalists. This is not a wild idea; journalists who are designated education reporters have told me that they would welcome this. It would require investment, but given the precarious, fake-news agenda of the past few years, there is an opportunity to demonstrate how education reporting is grounded in trusted research.

Such education would be underpinned by the collective social characteristics relevant to assessment, using evidence from teachers and from students, and including evidence from broader research in public settings. It is the collective investment and interactions born out of this kind of approach that will improve confidence and trust, and so help us to move towards reshaping of discourses.

Social media

I have thought for a long time about how we address those discourses of doom, desire and everything in between that flow in a steady stream across social media. My conclusion is that we have to agree that what happens there is not possible to control. Attempting to challenge or change minds in social media spaces is a waste of our time; it is like shouting into a black hole.

My advice here is to discuss issues relating to assessment on social media platforms if you wish, but don't expect to use these forums as a place to enact change. The clue is in the descriptor – they are social spaces, not educative spaces. What happens on some social media platforms might provide a means of glimpsing what is important to students at particular moments, and the growing body of research in this regard may well be able to feed into future discourses. My advice? What happens on social media stays on social media.

Students

Students – those who really do matter, those most profoundly impacted by the outcomes of assessments – are often at the mercy of public discourses that scrutinise the results of high-stakes testing, seeking error and unrest. Of course, where genuine mistakes occur, then there should be reparation, but there is something else – more profound and not easy to take. Difficulties need to be faced, in education as in life itself.

Such ideas are rooted in the earliest philosophical accounts, as Suissa (2008: 587) explains: 'a powerful and central part of all pictures of education since Plato involves the idea that for something to be truly educational it must be challenging, unsettling.' She is not arguing that there is something noble in the experience of suffering; rather, to appreciate how learning can change us and, in doing so, broaden our life experiences. Suissa (2008: 260) continues:

> To offer children straightforward, comfortable and unchallenging learning experiences is to deny them the excitement – and the

risks – of a truly educational experience, and thus to deprive them of the encounter with what [Martha] Nussbaum describes as 'the messy, unclear stuff of which our humanity is made'.

That messy and complex nature of humanity reflects my argument that assessment itself is a complex and murky terrain to negotiate, and that attempts to simplify what it is and how it functions are problematic. They dilute (or even prevent) opportunities to learn and, in so doing, they reduce opportunities to build confidence in the systems.

One final point in relation to the shaping of students: keeping the idea of assessment dysmorphia in our practice and in all assessment discourses is vital. It is important that educators, parents and students are aware of the signs of assessment anxiety and know where to access support. This acknowledgement of the stress has to be balanced with two things: first, ensuring that we don't constantly remind students, teachers and parents to be worried about tests; and second, understanding how we have normalised this competitive testing industry, with its stress on students, schools and scarce resources. Is there any value in continuing with the pressure and competition?

Our way of defining and managing discourses becomes a habit that we are reluctant to change. Even when presented with strong evidence to the contrary, we prefer to remain where we are because, as Garrison *et al.* (2012) argue, it's easy and comfortable to remain with an established value, doctrine or way of thinking. They found that habits tend to fix beliefs more firmly. Habits can actually 'arrest intellectual life' (Garrison *et al.*, 2012: 453) to the extent that we will avoid facing anything that is beyond our understanding.

However, guided by evidence-based research we can face those demons and the positive side to developing confidence in education. Masschelein and Simons (2015: 83) sum up the capacity to change in this claim:

> The assumption of our school morphology is simple in this regard: the school is a historical invention, and can therefore disappear. But this also means that the school can be reinvented (and re-decided), and that is precisely what we see as our challenge and as our responsibility today.

So, we can take this idea and remodel it – the assessments we have had in the past don't need to be the ones that we have in the future. Surely we deserve to think of new and innovative ways to work, to learn and to evolve? The last years during numerous lockdowns, homeschooling, changes to working practice and our very lived experiences have demonstrated not only our precarity and fragility, but also our resilience and resourcefulness. Reports summarising global responses to the pandemic through 2020 and beyond reveal remarkable innovation in the responses of educators to the COVID-19 crisis, with those systems most engaged with families and communities showing the greatest resilience. We must encourage conditions that give frontline educators autonomy and flexibility to act collaboratively (UNESCO, 2020).

Final thoughts

Public understanding of assessment remains rarely discussed globally, yet the key outcomes related to assessment are continuously scrutinised and analysed in all public domains via news channels, newspapers, social media and other online forums. What is apparent from only a brief look at these information channels is how poor the understanding of educational assessment actually is – and also how little access there is to good, clear information on the topic. There is a problem and those stakeholders invested in managing educational assessment (from policymakers to exam boards and schools) do very little to improve the situation.

Living in a so-called information age, where everyone, technically, has access to anything, clashes with a chilly climate, where the expert is sometimes treated with suspicion and derision. It has been said that we can all be experts now, because Google will tell us what we need to know. But is just knowing something enough?

In the case of educational assessment, good information is often hard to find. Even when it has been dug out, it can be baffling, confusing, confused and commonly riddled with misinformation – and I say this as a so-called expert in assessment! The problem of confidence and confusion about assessment does not just reveal itself in public domains; there is also a problem in schools that is leaking into society. This is not fake news; there is evidence of the negative impact of over-testing, increased mental health reporting, high levels of students/teacher anxiety and parental concerns. These issues appear to lack solutions. Instead, the policies from education policymakers around the world continue to champion a continuously narrowing curriculum – more tests that are deemed to meet that elusive 'gold standard' or even higher levels of rigour (namely, that are more difficult).

Such competition nurtures a culture in schools that is based on punitive responses to failure or underperformance for both teachers and their students. On the one hand, the idea of failure is problematic and something to be avoided at all costs; but on the other, students are urged to be resilient to failure, to adapt and to accept. These clashing messages can establish unrealistic expectations and precipitate kneejerk reactions when things don't go as expected. I continue to be disturbed by how a minority of assessments shape our lives and our children's lives.

However, I am confident and hopeful of change, because it can happen. Just to repeat a message to readers who might be skimming this text: *I am not anti-testing or opposed to examinations as a form of assessment.* As Berry (2017) declares, tests need to be put in their place, so teachers can be more creative and students can be more confident learners. The intention of this book is to start the conversation about how we do things differently in assessment, and how we can change what is clearly not always working.

In the words of many of my own school reports: 'Could try harder'. If we all tried harder, we might change this. Then teenage girls (like the one mentioned in the Introduction) might not feel the need to write letters to Santa, asking for good grades instead of real gifts.

References

Abdollahi, A., Carlbring, P., Vaez, E. and Ghahfarokhi, S. A. (2018) 'Perfectionism and test anxiety among high-school students: The moderating role of academic hardiness'. *Current Psychology*, 37 (3), 632–9. doi:10.1007/s12144-016-9550-z.

Abu-Ouf, N. M. and Jan, M. M. (2014) 'The influence of fish oil on neurological development and function'. *The Canadian Journal of Neurological Sciences/Le journal canadien des sciences neurologiques*, 41 (1), 13–18. doi:10.1017/S031716710001619X.

Adams, R. (2017) 'Eton pupils' marks disallowed over second exam paper leak', *The Guardian*, 30 August. Accessed 27 November 2021. https://www.theguardian.com/education/2017/aug/30/eton-pupils-marks-disallowed-over-second-exam-paper-leak.

Aksoy, M. E. (2018) 'A qualitative study on the reasons for social media addiction'. *European Journal of Educational Research*, 7(4), 861–5. doi:10.12973/eu-jer.7.4.861.

Al-Ghannami, S. S., Al-Adawi, S., Ghebremeskel, K., Hussein, I. S., Min, Y., Jeyaseelan, L. and Al-Oufi, H. S. (2019) 'Randomized open-label trial of docosahexaenoic acid–enriched fish oil and fish meal on cognitive and behavioral functioning in Omani children'. *Nutrition*, 57, 167–72. doi:10.1016/j.nut.2018.04.008.

Alexander, J. and Black, R. (2015) 'Educational testing in dystopian young adult fiction'. *Children's Literature*, 43 (1), 208–34.

Almog, T. and Almog, O. (2019) *Generation Y: Generation Snowflake?* London: Vallentine Mitchell.

Amaral, A. and Rosa, M. J. (eds) (2014) *Quality Assurance in Higher Education: Contemporary Debates*. Basingstoke: Palgrave Macmillan.

Amaral, M. P. do, Steiner-Khamsi, G. and Thompson, C. (eds) (2019) *Researching the Global Education Industry: Commodification, the market and business involvement*. Cham: Palgrave.

American Educational Research Association, American Psychological Association, and National Council on Measurement in Education (eds) (2014) *Standards for Educational and Psychological Testing*. Lanham, MD: American Educational Research Association

Andrade, H. L., Bennett, R. E. and Cizek, G. J. (eds) (2019) *Handbook of Formative Assessment in the Disciplines*. London: Routledge.

Apple, M. (2009) 'Is there a place for education in social transformation?', in H. S. Shapiro (ed.), *Education and Hope in Troubled Times*. Abingdon: Routledge.

AQA (2021a) *AQA Research and Analysis*. Accessed 27 November 2021. https://www.aqa.org.uk/about-us/our-research.

AQA (2021b) 'How a question paper is created'. Accessed 27 November 2021. https://www.aqa.org.uk/about-us/what-we-do/getting-the-right-result/how-exams-work/making-an-exam-a-guide-to-creating-a-question-paper.

Assessment Reform Group and University of Cambridge (2002) *Testing, Motivation and Learning*. Cambridge: University of Cambridge, Faculty of Education.

Atkinson, D. (2012) 'Contemporary art and art in education: The new, emancipation and truth'. *International Journal of Art & Design Education*, 31 (1), 5–18.

Atkinson, D. (2018) *Art, Disobedience, and Ethics: The adventure of pedagogy*. Cham: Springer International.

Bagley, J. J. (ed.) (1969) *The State and Education in England and Wales, 1833–1968*. London: Macmillan.

Baird, J.-A. and Gray, L. (2016) 'The meaning of curriculum-related examination standards in Scotland and England: a home–international comparison'. *Oxford Review of Education*, 42 (3), 266–84. doi:10.1080/03054985.2016.1184866.

Baird, J.-A., Isaacs, T., Opposs, D. and Grey, L. (eds) (2018) *Examination Standards: How measures and meanings differ around the world*. London: IOE Press.

Ball, S. J. (2001) '"You've been NERFed!" Dumbing down the academy: National Educational Research Forum: "A national strategy? Consultation paper": A brief and bilious response'. *Journal of Education Policy*, 16 (3), 265–8.

Ball, S. J. (2003) 'The teacher's soul and the terrors of performativity'. *Journal of Education Policy*, 18 (2), 215–28.

Ball, S. J. (2017) *The Education Debate* (3rd edn). Bristol: Policy Press.

Ball, S. J. (2018) 'Global education policy: Reform and profit'. *Revista de Estudios Teóricos y Epistemológicos en Política Educativa*, 3 (January), 1–14. doi:10.5212/retepe.v.3.015.

Ball, S. J. and Junemann, C. (2012) *Networks, New Governance and Education*. Bristol: Policy Press.

Bauer, M. W. and Gaskell, G. (2000) *Qualitative Researching with Text, Image and Sound*. London: SAGE Publications. doi:10.4135/9781849209731.

BBC News (2015) 'India arrests hundreds over Bihar school cheating', *BBC News online*, 21 March. Accessed 27 November 2021. https://www.bbc.co.uk/news/world-asia-31998343.

Bearman, M., Dawson, P., Bennett, S., Hall, M., Molloy, E., Boud, D. and Joughin, G. (2017) 'How university teachers design assessments: A cross-disciplinary study'. *Higher Education*, 74 (1), 49–64. doi:1

Bennett, S., Maton, K. and Kervin, L. (2010) 'The digital natives debate: A critical review of the evidence'. *British Journal of Educational Technology*, 39 (5), 775–86. doi:10.1111/j.1467-8535.2007.00793.x.

Berger, J. (ed.) (1972) *Ways of Seeing / Based on the BBC television series with John Berger; a book made by John Berger ... [et al.]*. London: British Broadcasting Corporation and Penguin.

Berger, J. (2008) *Ways of Seeing: John Berger*. London: BBC, Penguin.

Berners-Lee, T. (2020) 'Covid-19 makes it clearer than ever: Access to the internet should be a universal right', *The Guardian*, 4 June. Accessed 27 November 2021, https://www.theguardian.com/commentisfree/2020/jun/04/covid-19-internet-universal-right-lockdown-online.

Berry, J. (2017) *Putting the Test in its Place: Teaching well and keeping the number crunchers quiet*. London: IOE Press.

Biesta, G. (2015) 'What is education for? On good education, teacher judgement, and educational professionalism'. *European Journal of Education*, 50 (1), 75–87. doi:10.1111/ejed.12109.

Billingham, S. (ed.) (2018) *Access to Success and Social Mobility Through Higher Education: A curate's egg?* Bingley: Emerald.

Binet, A. and Simon, T. H. (1916) *The Development of Intelligence in Children (the Binet-Simon scale)*. T. Simon and E. S. Kite (eds). Baltimore: Williams & Wilkins company.

Black, P. (1988) *National Curriculum: Task Group on Assessment and Testing report: A digest for schools*. London: Department of Education and Science, Welsh Office.

Black, P. (2013) *Inside the Black Box of Assessment: Assessment of learning by teachers and schools*. London: GL Assessment.

Black, P. (2014) *Testing: Friend or foe?* London: Routledge.

Black, P., Harrison, C., Lee, C., Marshall, B. and Wiliam, D. (2003) *Assessment for Learning: Putting it into practice*. Maidenhead: Open University Press.

Black, P. and Wiliam, D. (1998) 'Assessment and classroom learning'. *Assessment in Education: Principles, Policy & Practice*, 5 (1), 7–74. doi:10.1080/0969595980050102.

Black, P. and Wiliam, D. (2018) 'Classroom assessment and pedagogy'. *Assessment in Education: Principles, policy and practice*, 25 (6), 551–75. doi:10.1080/0969594X.2018.1441807.

Block, N. J. and Dworkin, G. (eds) (1977) *The IQ Controversy: Critical readings*. London: Quartet Books.

Bloodworth, J. (2016) *The Myth of Meritocracy*. London: Biteback Publications.

Bloxham, S. and Price, M. (2016) 'Let's stop the pretence of consistent marking: Exploring the multiple limitations of assessment criteria'. *Assessment and Evaluation in Higher Education*, 41 (3). doi:10.1080/02602938.2015.1024607.

Blyton, E. (1941) *The Twins at St Clares*. London: Methuen.

Blyton, E. (1948) *The Second Form at Malory Towers*. London: Methuen.

Bolton, P. (2012) *Education: Historical statistics*. Research Briefing, 27 November. Accessed 19 January 2022. https://researchbriefings.files.parliament.uk/documents/SN04252/SN04252.pdf.

Boud, D. (ed.) (1988) *Developing Student Autonomy in Learning* (2nd edn). London: Kogan Page.

Boud, D. (2000) 'Sustainable assessment: Rethinking assessment for the learning society'. *Studies in Continuing Education*, 22 (2), 151–67. doi:10.1080/713695728.

Boud, D., Freeman, M., James, R., Joughin, G., Sadler, R., Dochy, F. and Fitzgerald, T. (2010) *Student Assessment for Learning in and after Courses*. Sydney: Australian Learning and Teaching Council.

Boud, D. and Soler, R. (2016) 'Sustainable assessment revisited'. *Assessment & Evaluation in Higher Education*, 41 (3), 400–13. doi:10.1080/02602938.2015.1018133.

Bourke, B. (2019) 'Connecting with Generation Z through social media', in H. L. Schnackenberg and C. Johnson (eds), *Preparing the Higher Education Space for Gen Z*. Hershey, PA: IGI Global, 124–47. doi:10.4018/978-1-5225-7763-8.ch007.

Bourke, R. and Mentis, M. (2014) 'An assessment framework for inclusive education: integrating assessment approaches'. *Assessment in Education: Principles, Policy & Practice*, 21 (4), 384–97. doi:10.1080/0969594X.2014.888332.

Bradbury, A. (2018) 'The impact of the phonics screening check on grouping by ability: A "necessary evil" amid the policy storm'. *British Educational Research Journal*, 44 (4), 539–56. doi:10.1002/berj.3449.

Bradbury, A. and Roberts-Holmes, G. (2018) *The Datafication of Primary and Early Years Education: Playing with numbers*. London: Routledge.

Braun, J. and Gillespie, T. (2011) 'Hosting the public discourse, hosting the public: When online news and social media converge'. *Journalism Practice*, 5 (4), 383–98. doi:10.1080/17512786.2011.557560.

Briant, E. L. and Wanless, A. (2019) 'A digital ménage à trois', in C. Bjola and J. Pamment (eds), *Countering Online Propaganda and Extremism*. London: Routledge, 44–65. doi:10.4324/9781351264082-4.

Brighouse, H. (2006) *On Education*. London: Routledge.

Britton, J., Farquharson, C., Sibieta, L., Tahir, I. and Waltmann, B. (2020) *2020 Annual Report on Education Spending in England. R183*. London: Institute for Fiscal Studies.

Broadfoot, P. (1998) 'Records of achievement and the learning society: A tale of two discourses', *Assessment in Education: Principles, policy & practice*, 5 (3), 447–77. doi:10.1080/0969595980050307.

Broadfoot, P. (2007) *An Introduction to Assessment*. London: Continuum.

Broadfoot, P. and Pollard, A. (2006) 'The changing discourse of assessment policy: The case of English primary education', in H. Lauder, P. Brown, J.-A. Dillabough, and A. H. Halsey (eds), *Education, Globalization & Social Change*. New York: Oxford University Press.

Brown, G. T. L. (2018) *Assessment of Student Achievement*. New York: Routledge.

Brown, G. T. L. (2004) 'Teachers' conceptions of assessment: Implications for policy and professional development'. *Assessment in Education: Principles, Policy & Practice*, 11 (3), 301–18. doi:10.1080/0969594042000304609.

Brown, G. T. L. and Hirschfield, G. H. F. (2009) 'Students' conceptions of assessment: Links to outcomes'. *Assessment in Education: Principles, policy & practice*, 15 (1), 3–17. doi: http://dx.doi.org/10.1080/09695940701884636.

Brown, G. T. L., Hui, S. K. F., Yu, F. W. M. and Kennedy, K. J. (2011) 'Teachers' conceptions of assessment in Chinese contexts: A tripartite model of accountability, improvement, and irrelevance'. *International Journal of Educational Research*, 50 (5), 307–20. doi:10.1016/j.ijer.2011.10.003.

Brown, S. and Race, P. (2012) 'Using effective assessment to promote learning', in L. Hunt and D. Chalmers (eds), *University Teaching in Focus: A learning-centred approach*, London: Routledge, 74–91.

Buglass, S. L., Binder, J. F., Betts, L. R. and Underwood, J. D. M. (2016) 'Motivators of online vulnerability: The impact of social network site use and FOMO'. *Computers in Human Behavior*, 66, 248–55. doi:10.1016/j.chb.2016.09.055.

Busby, M. (2019) 'Graduate receives £61,000 over "Mickey Mouse degree" claim', *The Guardian*, 2 June. Accessed 27 November 2021. https://www.theguardian.com/uk-news/2019/jun/02/graduate-who-sued-university-says-payout-barely-covers-her-costs.

Butler, K. and Reynolds, K. (2014) *Modern Children's Literature* (2nd edn). London: Palgrave.

Campbell, R. J. (1993) 'The broad and balanced curriculum in primary schools: Some limitations on reform'. *The Curriculum Journal*, 4 (2), 215–29. doi:10.1080/0958517930040204.

Carless, D. (2009) 'Trust, distrust and their impact on assessment reform'. *Assessment & Evaluation in Higher Education*, 34 (1), 79–89. doi:10.1080/02602930801895786.

Carless, D. (2020) 'Double duty, shared responsibilities and feedback literacy'. *Perspectives on Medical Education*, 9 (4), 199–200. doi:10.1007/s40037-020-00599-9.

Carroll, L. (2015) *Alice's Adventures in Wonderland: 150th anniversary edition*. Banchoff, T., Burstein, M. and Dalí, S. (eds). Princeton: Princeton University Press.

Chamberlain, S. (2013) 'Communication strategies for enhancing qualification users' understanding of educational assessment: Recommendations from other public interest fields'. *Oxford Review of Education*, 39 (1), 114–27. doi:10.1080/03054985.2013.764757.

Chandler, D. and Munday, R. (2016) *Oversharing*. Oxford: Oxford University Press.

Charbonneau, J. (2013) *The Testing*. Boston: Houghton Mifflin Harcourt.

Cheng, L., Klinger, D., Fox, J., Doe, C., Jin, Y. and Wu, J. (2014) 'Motivation and test anxiety in test performance across three testing contexts: The CAEL, CET, and GEPT'. *TESOL Quarterly*, 48 (2), 300–30. doi:10.1002/tesq.105.

Child, L. (2004) *Clarice Bean Spells Trouble*. London: Orchard Books.

Cianciolo, A. T. (2004) *Intelligence: A brief history*. Malden, MA: Blackwell.

Clarke, S. (2020) *A Little Guide for Teachers: Formative assessment*. London: Corwin Press.

Coates, S. and Lay, K. (2018) 'Self-harming by teenage girls doubles in 20 years'. *The Times*, 6 August. Accessed 9 January 2022. https://www.thetimes.co.uk/article/self-harming-by-teenage-girls-doubles-in-20-years-x2vbzm87m.

Collins, S. (2011) *The Hunger Games*. London: Scholastic.

Cook, J., DuFalla, A. and National Center for Youth Issues (2014) *The Anti-Test Anxiety Society*. Chattanooga TN: National Centre for Youth Studies. Accessed 11 January 2022. https://ncyi.org/product/the-anti-test-anxiety-society/.

Crawford, C. (2014) *Socio-economic differences in university outcomes in the UK: Drop-out, degree completion and degree class*. IFS Working Paper W14/31. doi:10.1920/wp.ifs.2014.1431.

Cresswell, M. (2000) 'The role of public examinations in defining and monitoring standards'. In H. Goldstein and A. Heath (eds), *Educational Standards* (Proceedings of the British Academy 102): Oxford: Oxford University Press, 69–120.

Crittenden, V. L., Hanna, R. C. and Peterson, R. A. (2009) 'The cheating culture: A global societal phenomenon'. *Business Horizons*, 52, 337–46. doi:10.1016/j.bushor.2009.02.004.

Crook, D. and McCulloch, G. (eds) (2008) *The Routledge International Encyclopedia of Education*. London: Routledge.

Cummings, W. K. and Bain, O. (2017) 'Modeling strategies for enhancing educational quality'. *Research in Comparative and International Education*, 12 (2), 160–73. doi:10.1177/1745499917711546.

Curtis, S. J. and Boultwood, M. E. A. (1962) *An Introductory History of English Education since 1800* (2nd edn). London: University Tutorial Press.

D'Agostino, A., Schirripa Spagnolo, F. and Salvati, N. (2021) 'Studying the relationship between anxiety and school achievement: evidence from PISA data'. *Statistical Methods & Applications*. doi:10.1007/s10260-021-00563-9.

Dahl, R. (1988) *Matilda*. London: Jonathan Cape.

Damla Kentli, F. (2009) 'Comparison of hidden curriculum theories'. *European Journal of Educational Studies*, 1 (2), 83–88.

Dann, R. (2002) *Promoting Assessment as Learning: Improving the learning process*. London: RoutledgeFalmer.

Dann, R. (2014) 'Assessment as learning: Blurring the boundaries of assessment and learning for theory, policy and practice'. *Assessment in Education: Principles, policy & practice*, 21 (2), 149–66. doi:10.1080/0969594X.2014.898128.

Dann, R. (2018) *Developing Feedback for Pupil Learning: Teaching, learning and assessment in schools*. London: Routledge.

Davies, N. (2011) *Flat Earth News: An award-winning reporter exposes falsehood, distortion and propaganda in the global media*. London: Random House.

Davis, W. (2016) *Fake or real? How to self-check the news and get the facts: All tech considered*. Accessed 11 January 2022 https://www.npr.org/sections/alltechconsidered/2016/12/05/503581220/fake-or-real-how-to-self-check-the-news-and-get-the-facts?t=1641724335008.

Day, E. (2019) *How to Fail*. Accessed 11 January 2022. https://howtofail.podbean.com/.

Deneen, C. and Boud, D. (2014) 'Patterns of resistance in managing assessment change'. *Assessment and Evaluation in Higher Education*, 39 (5), 577–91. doi:10.1080/02602938.2013.859654.

Deng, Z. (2020) *Knowledge, Content, Curriculum and Didaktik: Beyond social realism*. London: Taylor & Francis.

Department for Education (2018) *Assessment and Standards Update Response and Guidance*, 18 December. Accessed 9 January 2022. https://www.gov.uk/government/publications/sta-assessment-update-18-december-2018.

Department for Education (2019) *Participation Rates in Higher Education: 2006/2007 to 2017/ 2018*, 27 September 2021. Accessed 27 November 2021 https://www.gov.uk/government/ statistics/participation-rates-in-higher-education-2006-to-2017.

Dewey, J. (1910) *How We Think*. Boston: D.C. Heath & Co.

Dewey, J. (1915) *The School and Society* (2nd edn). Chicago: University of Chicago Press.

Dhawan, V. and Zanini, N. (2014) 'Big Data and social media analytics'. *Research Matters: A Cambridge Assessment publication*, 18, 36–41.

Donolato, E., Marci, T., Altoè, G. and Mammarella, I. C. (2020) 'Measuring test anxiety in primary and middle school children'. *European Journal of Psychological Assessment: Official organ of the European Association of Psychological Assessment*, 36 (5), 839–51. doi:10.1027/1015-5759/ a000556.

Dredge, S. (2018) 'Mobile phone addiction? It's time to take back control', *The Guardian*, 27 January. Accessed 27 November 2021. https://www.theguardian.com/technology/2018/ jan/27/mobile-phone-addiction-apps-break-the-habit-take-back-control.

Du Sautoy, M. (2019) *The Creativity Code*. Cambridge, MA: The Belknap Press of Harvard University Press.

Dweck, C. S. (2015) 'Growth mindset, revisited'. *Education Week*, 35 (5), 20–4. doi:10.1017/ CBO9781107415324.004.

Eckstein, M. A. (2003) *Combating Academic Fraud: Towards a culture of integrity*. Paris: International Institute for Educational Planning.

The Economist (2016) 'Generation screwed or generation snowflake? Britain's young are doing better than many think', 19 November. Accessed 25 March 2022. https://www.economist. com/britain/2016/11/17/britains-young-are-doing-better-than-many-think.

The Economist (2021) 'Education in China is becoming increasingly unfair to the poor', 29 May, 54–55. Accessed 27 November 2021. https://www.economist.com/china/2021/05/27/ education-in-china-is-becoming-increasingly-unfair-to-the-poor.

Education Services Australia (2016) *NAP - NAPLAN - general*. Accessed 27 November 2021. https:// www.nap.edu.au/naplan/faqs/naplan--general.

Elmqvist, K. O., Rigaudy, M. T. and Vink, J. P. (2016) 'Creating a no-blame culture through medical education: A UK perspective'. *Journal of Multidisciplinary Healthcare*, 9, 345–6. doi:10.2147/ JMDH.S111813.

Entwisle, D. R. and Hayduk, L. (1978) *Too Great Expectations: The academic outlook of young children*. Baltimore: Johns Hopkins University Press.

Entwistle, N. and Ramsden, P. (2015) *Understanding Student Learning*. London: Routledge.

Esmonde, I. and Booker, A. N. (2017) *Power and Privilege in the Learning Sciences: Critical and socio-cultural theories of learning*. London: Routledge.

European Commission (2018) *A Multi-dimensional Approach to Disinformation: Report of the independent high level group on fake news and online disinformation*. Luxembourg.

Eurostat (2019) *Being Young in Europe Today – Digital world*. Accessed 27 November 2021. https:// ec.europa.eu/eurostat/statistics-explained/index.php/Being_young_in_Europe_today_-_di gital_world#A_digital_age_divide.

Evans, B. and Waites, B. (1981) *IQ and Mental Testing: An unnatural science and its social history*. London: Macmillan.

Eysenck, M. W. (1979) 'Anxiety, learning, and memory: A reconceptualization'. *Journal of Research in Personality*, 13 (4), 363–85. doi:10.1016/0092-6566(79)90001-1.

Fagg, S. (1990) *Entitlement for All in Practice: A broad, balanced & relevant curriculum for children & young people with severe & complex learning difficulties in the 1990s*. London: David Fulton.

Fielding, M. (2011) 'Patterns of partnership: Student voice, intergenerational learning and demo-cratic fellowship', in N. Mockler and J. Sachs (eds), *Rethinking Educational Practice Through Reflexive Inquiry*. Dordrecht: Springer, 61–75.

Finchler, J. and O'Malley, K. (2003) *Testing Miss Malarkey*. New York: Walker & Co.

Fiore, L. B. (2012) *Assessment of Young Children: A collaborative approach*. New York: Routledge.

Fleer, M. (2015) 'Developing an assessment pedagogy: The tensions and struggles in re-theorising assessment from a cultural–historical perspective'. *Assessment in Education: Principles, policy and practice*, 22 (2), 224–46. doi:10.1080/0969594X.2015.1015403.

Forkuor, J. B., Amarteifio, J., Attoh, D. O. and Buari, M.A. (2018) 'Students' perception of cheat-ing and the best time to cheat during examinations'. *The Urban Review*, 51 (3), 424–43. doi:10.1007/s11256-018-0491-8.

Fortune Business Insights (2021) *Private Tutoring Market Size, Share & COVID-19 Impact Analysis, By Subjects (Academic and Non-academic), Application (Up-to K-12 and Post K-12), Mode (Offline and Online), and Regional Forecast, 2021–2028*. Accessed 27 November 2021. https://www.fortunebusinessinsights.com/toc/private-tutoring-market-104753.

Foucault, M. (1972) *The Archaeology of Knowledge: And the discourse on language*. A. M. Sheridan Smith (trans.). New York: Pantheon Books.

Franke, W. (1972) *The Reform and Abolition of the Traditional Chinese Examination System*. Cambridge, MA: Harvard University Press.

Furedi, F. (2010) 'Introduction to the marketisation of higher education and the student as consumer', in M. Molesworth, R. Scullion and E. Nixon (eds), *The Marketisation of Higher Education and the Student as Consumer*. London: Taylor and Francis, 1–8.

Gajda, A. (2009) *The Trials of Academe: The New Era of Campus Litigation*. Cambridge, MA: Harvard University Press.

Gardner, J. (2016) *The Public Understanding of Assessment*. London: Routledge.

Garrison, J., Neubert, S. and Reich, K. (2012) 'Education and Culture – The cultural turn', in *John Dewey's Philosophy of Education: An introduction and recontextualization for our times*. New York: Palgrave Macmillan, 1–40. doi:10.1057/9781137026187_1.

Gedye, S., Fender, E. and Chalkley, B. (2007) 'Undergraduate expectations and post-graduation experiences of the value of a degree'. *Journal of Geography in Higher Education*, 28 (3), 381–96. doi:10.1080/0309826042000286956.

Gewin, V. (2021) 'Pandemic burnout is rampant in academia'. *Nature*, 591, 491–3 doi:10.1038/d41586-021-00663-2.

Gibson, T. A. (2018) 'The post-truth double helix: Reflexivity and mistrust in local politics', *International Journal of Communication*, 12, 3167–85.

Gillett, K. (2012) 'A critical discourse analysis of British national newspaper representations of the academic level of nurse education: too clever for our own good?'. *Nursing Inquiry*, 19 (4), 297–307. doi:10.1111/j.1440-1800.2011.00564.x.

Gillett, K. (2014) 'Nostalgic constructions of nurse education in British national newspapers'. *Journal of Advanced Nursing*, 70 (11), 2495–505.

Gipps, C. (1994) *Beyond Testing*. London: Routledge.

Gipps, C. (2012) *Beyond Testing* (2nd edn). London: Routledge.

Goodhart, C. A. E. (1984) *Monetary Theory and Practice: The UK experience*. London: Macmillan.

Grant, K. B. and Ray, J. A. (2010) *Home, School, and Community Collaboration: Culturally responsive family involvement*. Thousand Oaks: SAGE Publications.

Green, A. (2013) *Education and State Formation Europe, East Asia and the USA* (2nd edn). Basingstoke: Palgrave Macmillan.

Griffin, P., Care, E. and McGaw, B. (2012) 'The changing role of education and schools', in P. Griffin, B. McGaw and E. Care (eds), *Assessment and Teaching of 21st Century Skills*. Dordrecht: Springer, 1–15. doi:10.1007/978-94-007-2324-5_1.

Gruner, E. R. (2009) 'Teach the children: Education and knowledge in recent children's fantasy'. *Children's Literature*, 37 (1), 216–35.

Haand, R. and Shuwang, Z. (2020) 'The relationship between social media addiction and depression: A quantitative study among university students in Khost, Afghanistan'. *International Journal of Adolescence and Youth*, 25 (1). doi:10.1080/02673843.2020.1741407.

Habermas, J. (2006) 'Political communication in media society: Does democracy still enjoy an epistemic dimension? The impact of normative theory on empirical research', *Communication Theory*, 16 (4), 411–26.

Hall, D., James, D. and Marsden, N. (2012) 'Marginal gains: Olympic lessons in high performance for organisations'. *HR Bulletin: Research and practice*, 7 (2), 9–13.

Harding, A. F. (2000) *European Societies in the Bronze Age*. Cambridge: Cambridge University Press. doi:10.1017/cbo9780511605901.

Harlen, W. (ed.) (2008) *Student Assessment and Testing*. Los Angeles: SAGE Publications.

HarperCollins (n.d.) 'Fake News'. *Collins English Dictionary*. Accessed 25 march 2022. https://www.collinsdictionary.com/dictionary/english/fake-news.

Harris, J., Zhao, Y. and Caldwell, B. J. (2009) 'Global characteristics of school transformation in China'. *Asia Pacific Journal of Education*, 29 (4), 413–26. doi:10.1080/02188790903308860.

Harris, K. (1999) 'Aims, whose aims?', in R. Marples (ed.), *The Aims of Education*. London: Routledge, 1–13.

Hattie, J. (2007) 'The power of feedback'. *Review of Educational Research*, 77 (1), 81–112.

Hattie, J. and Brown, G. T. L. (2010) 'Assessment and evaluation', in C. Rubie-Davies (ed.), *Educational Psychology: Concepts, research and challenges*. London: Routledge, 102–17. doi:10.4324/9780203838884.

Hattie, J. and Timperley, H. (2007) 'The power of feedback'. *Review of Educational Research*, 77 (1), 81–112. doi:10.3102/003465430298487.

Have, S., Rijsman, J., Have, W. and Westhof, J. (eds) (2018) *The Social Psychology of Change Management*. London: Routledge.

Hembree, R. (1988) 'Correlates, causes, effects, and treatment of test anxiety'. *Review of Educational Research*, 58 (1), 47–77.

Henn, T. R. (1951) 'Causes of failure in examinations'. *British Medical Journal*, 2 (56), 461–4.

Hern, A. (2017) 'Facebook and Twitter are being used to manipulate public opinion – report', *The Guardian*, 19 June. Accessed 27 November 2021. https://www.theguardian.com/technol ogy/2017/jun/19/social-media-proganda-manipulating-public-opinion-bots-accounts-faceb ook-twitter.

Hern, A. (2021) 'Smartphone is now "the place where we live", anthropologists say', *The Guardian*, 10 May. Accessed 27 November 2021. https://www.theguardian.com/technology/2021/ may/10/smartphone-is-now-the-place-where-we-live-anthropologists-say.

HESA (Higher Education Statistics Agency) (2021) 'What are HE students' progression rates and qualifications?' Accessed 27 November 2021. https://www.hesa.ac.uk/data-and-analysis/ students/outcomes#classifications.

Hill, K. T. (1967) 'Social reinforcement as a function of test anxiety and success-failure experiences'. *Child Development*, 38 (3), 723. doi:10.2307/1127250.

Hill, K. T. and Eaton, W. O. (1977) 'The interaction of test anxiety and success-failure experiences in determining children's arithmetic performance'. *Developmental Psychology*, 13 (3), 205–11. doi:10.1037/0012-1649.13.3.205.

Hill, K. T. and Sarason, S. B. (1966) 'The relation of test anxiety and defensiveness to test and school performance over the elementary-school years: A further longitudinal study'. *Monographs of the Society for Research in Child Development*, 31 (2), 1–76. doi:10.2307/1165770.

Hoferichter, F., Raufelder, D. and Eid, M. (2015) 'Socio-motivational moderators – two sides of the same coin? Testing the potential buffering role of socio-motivational relationships on achievement drive and test anxiety among German and Canadian secondary school students'. *Frontiers in Psychology*, 6. doi:10.3389/fpsyg.2015.01675.

Hornby, G. and Lafaele, R. (2011) 'Educational review barriers to parental involvement in education: an explanatory model'. *Educational Review*, 63 (1), 37–52. doi:10.1080/ 00131911.2010.488049.

Howe, M. J. A. (1997) *IQ in Question: The truth about intelligence*. London: SAGE Publications.

Howell, C. (2013) *Development and Analysis of a Measurement Scale for Teacher Assessment Literacy*. ProQuest Dissertations. Accessed 19 January 2022. http://search.proquest.com/docview/ 1411923246/.

Huang, Q., Peng, W. and Ahn, S. (2021) 'When media become the mirror: A meta-analysis on media and body image'. *Media Psychology*, 24 (4), 437–89. doi:10.1080/15213269.2020.1737545.

Independent Commission on Examination Malpractice (2019) *Report of the Independent Commission on Examination Malpractice presented to the Joint Council for Qualifications*. London: Independent Commission on Examination Malpractice.

International Association for the Evaluation of Educational Achievement (2017) *ILSA-Gateway: ILSA in Education*. Accessed 27 November 2021. https://ilsa-gateway.org/ilsa-in-education.

International Telecommunications Union (2019) *Measuring Digital Development: Facts and figures 2019*. Accessed 27 November 2021 https://www.itu.int/en/ITU-D/Statistics/Docume nts/facts/FactsFigures2019.pdf.

Isaacs, T. and Gorgen, K. (2018) 'Culture, context and controversy', in J.-A. Baird, T. Isaacs, D. Opposs and L. Grey (eds) *Examination Standards: How measure and meanings differ around the world*. London: IOE Press.

Jackson, P. W. (1968) *Life in Classrooms*. New York: Holt, Rinehart and Winston.

James, B. E. (2017) *Still Hidden, Still Ignored: Who cares for young carers*. London: Barnardo's. Accessed 19 January 2022. https://www.barnardos.org.uk/sites/default/files/uploads/still-hidden-still-ignored.pdf.

Jensen, K. and Walker, S. (2008) *Education, Democracy and Discourse*. London: Continuum.

Joint Council for Qualifications (2021a) *Examination System*. Accessed 27 November 2021. https://www.jcq.org.uk/examination-system/.

Joint Council for Qualifications (2021b) *Examiners and Marking*. Accessed 27 November 2021. https://www.jcq.org.uk/examination-system/the-role-of-an-examiner/.

Jones, L. V. and Thissen, D. (2006) 'History and overview of psychometrics', in C. R. Rao and S. Sinharay (eds), *Handbook of Statistics, 26: Psychometrics*. Amsterdam: Elsevier, 1–27. doi:10.1016/S0169-7161(06)26001-2.

Jones, M. (2019) 'The Gulf information war: Propaganda, fake news, and fake trends: The weaponization of Twitter bots in the Gulf Crisis'. *International Journal of Communication*, 13 (27), 1389–415.

Kairamo, K. (1989) *Education for Life: A European strategy* (European Roundtable Brussels and European Round Table of Industrialists). London: Butterworths.

Kajackaite, A. and Gneezy, U. (2017) 'Incentives and cheating'. *Games and Economic Behavior*, 102, 433–44. doi: https://doi.org/10.1016/j.geb.2017.01.015.

Kelly, A. V. (2009) *The Curriculum Theory and Practice* (6th edn). London: SAGE Publications.

Khaitan, A. S., Jeyanth, N., Kharbanda, N., Mankaran, D. and Shivani, N. J. (2017) *Online Education in India, 2021: A study by KPMG in India and Google*. Accessed 27 November 2021. https://assets.kpmg/content/dam/kpmg/in/pdf/2017/05/Online-Education-in-India-2021.pdf.

Kleemans, M., Daalmans, S., Carbaat, I. and Anschütz, D. (2018) 'Picture perfect: The direct effect of manipulated Instagram photos on body image in adolescent girls'. *Media Psychology*, 21 (1), 93–110. doi:10.1080/15213269.2016.1257392.

Klenowski, V. and Wyatt-Smith, C. (2012) 'The impact of high stakes testing: The Australian story'. *Assessment in Education: Principles, Policy and Practice*, 19 (1), 65–79. doi:10.1080/0969594X.2011.592972.

Konok, V., Gigler, D., Bereczky, B. M. and Miklósi, A. (2016) 'Humans' attachment to their mobile phones and its relationship with interpersonal attachment style', *Computers in Human Behavior*, 61, 537–47. doi:10.1016/j.chb.2016.03.062.

Koretz, D. M. (2008) *Measuring Up: What educational testing really tells us*. Cambridge, MA: Harvard University Press.

Kynaston, D. and Green, F. (2019) *Engines of Privilege: Britain's private school problem*. London: Bloomsbury.

Labaree, D. F. (2007) *Education, Markets, and the Public Good: The selected works of David F. Labaree*. London: Routledge.

Labaree, D. F. (2010) *Someone Has to Fail the Zero-sum Game of Public Schooling*. Cambridge, MA: Harvard University Press.

Lakoff, G. (1970) *Irregularity in Syntax*. New York: Holt, Rinehart and Winston.

Li, L. (2017) 'Recent trends and themes in realist Chinese children's fiction', in J. Stephens, C. A. Belmiro, A. Curry, L. Li and Y. S. Motawy (eds) *The Routledge Companion to International Children's Literature*. Abingdon: Routledge, 391–8. doi:10.4324/9781315771663.ch39.

Li, R., Kitchen, H., George, B., Richardson, M. and Fordham, E. (2019) *OECD Reviews of Evaluation and Assessment in Education: Georgia*. Paris: OECD.

Li, Y. and Ranieri, M. (2012) 'Are "digital natives" really digitally competent? – A study on Chinese teenagers'. *British Journal of Educational Technology*, 41 (6), 1029–42. doi:10.1111/j.1467-8535.2009.01053.x.

Lian, S. L., Sun, X. J., Niu, G. F., Yang, X. J., Zhou, Z. K. and Yang, C. (2021) 'Mobile phone addiction and psychological distress among Chinese adolescents: The mediating role of rumination and moderating role of the capacity to be alone'. *Journal of Affective Disorders*, 279, 701–10. doi:10.1016/j.jad.2020.10.005.

Lin, N. (2001) *Social Capital: A theory of social structure and action*. Cambridge: Cambridge University Press.

Liu, Q. Q., Zhou, Z. K., Yang, X. J., Kong, F. C., Niu, G. F. and Fan, C. Y. (2017) 'Mobile phone addiction and sleep quality among Chinese adolescents: A moderated mediation model'. *Computers in Human Behavior*, 72, 108–14. doi:10.1016/j.chb.2017.02.042.

Local News Singapore (2018) *Fewer exams, assessments in schools to reduce emphasis on academic results: MOE*, 28 September. Accessed 9 January 2022. https://localnewsingapore.com/fewer-exams-assessments-in-schools-to-reduce-emphasis-on-academic-results-moe/.

Lockwood, C. (2007) *The Human Story: Where we come from and how we evolved*. London: Natural History Museum.

Looney, A., Cumming, J., van Der Kleij, F. and Harris, K. (2017) 'Reconceptualising the role of teachers as assessors: Teacher assessment identity'. *Assessment in Education: Principles, Policy & Practice*, 25 (5), 442–67. doi:10.1080/0969594X.2016.1268090.

Lotz, C. and Sparfeldt, J. R. (2017) 'Does test anxiety increase as the exam draws near? – Students' state test anxiety recorded over the course of one semester'. *Personality and Individual Differences*, 104, 397–400. doi:10.1016/j.paid.2016.08.032.

Loughborough University (2017) 'Food refusal', *Child Feeding Guide*. Accessed 27 November 2021. https://www.childfeedingguide.co.uk/tips/common-feeding-pitfalls/food-refusal/.

Louie, B. Y.-Y. and Louie, D. H. (2002) 'Children's literature in the People's Republic of China: Its purposes and genres', in L. Wenling, J. S. Gaffney and J. L. Packard (eds), *Chinese Children's Reading Acquisition: Theoretical and pedagogical issues*. Boston, MA: Springer, 175–93. doi:10.1007/978-1-4615-0859-5_9.

Maguire, M., Ball, S. J. and Braun, A. (2011) *How Schools Do Policy*. London: Routledge.

Manjoo, F. (2018) 'Can Facebook, or anybody, solve the internet's misinformation problem?', *New York Times*, 22 August. Accessed 19 January 2022. https://www.nytimes.com/2018/08/22/technology/facebook-internet-misinformation.html.

Mansell, W. (2007) *Education by Numbers: The damaging treadmill of school tests*. London: Politico's.

Margaryan, A., Littlejohn, A. and Vojt, G. (2011) 'Are digital natives a myth or reality? University students' use of digital technologies'. *Computers and Education*, 56 (2), 429–40. doi:10.1016/j.compedu.2010.09.004.

Markus, K. A. and Borsboom, D. (2013) *Frontiers of Test Validity Theory*. London: Routledge. doi:10.4324/9780203501207.

Masschelein, J. and Simons, M. (2015) 'Education in times of fast learning: The future of the school'. *Ethics and Education*, 10 (1), 84–95. doi:10.1080/17449642.2014.998027.

Maxwell, C., Deppe, U., Krüger, H.-H. and Helsper, W. (eds) (2018) *Elite Education and Internationalisation: From the Early Years to higher education*. Cham: Springer International.

McAnany, E. G. (2014) 'Wilbur Schramm: Beginnings of the "communication" field'. *Communication Research Trends*, 33 (4), 3.

McDonald, A. S. (2001) 'The prevalence and effects of test anxiety in school children'. *Educational Psychology*, 21 (1), 89–101.

McMullen, D. L. (2011) 'The Chinese Examination System in Dynastic China: Did it select the brightest and best?'. *Sunway Academic Journal*, 8, 1–11.

Meadows, M. and Black, B. (2018) 'Teachers' experience of and attitudes toward activities to maximise qualification results in England'. *Oxford Review of Education*, 44 (5), 563–80. doi:10.1080/03054985.2018.1500355.

Medland, E. (2014) 'Assessment in higher education: Drivers, barriers and directions for change in the UK'. *Assessment & Evaluation in Higher Education*, 41 (1), 81–96. doi:10.1080/02602938.2014.982072.

Medland, E. (2015) 'Examining the assessment literacy of external examiners'. *London Review of Education*, 13 (3), 21–33. doi:10.18546/LRE.13.3.04.

Medland, E. (2016) 'Assessment in higher education: Drivers, barriers and directions for change in the UK'. *Assessment and Evaluation in Higher Education*, 41 (1), 81–96. doi:10.1080/02602938.2014.982072.

Medland, E. (2019) '"I'm an assessment illiterate": Towards a shared discourse of assessment literacy for external examiners'. *Assessment and Evaluation in Higher Education*, 44 (4), 565–80. doi:10.1080/02602938.2018.1523363.

Mihailidis, P. and Viotty, S. (2017) 'Spreadable spectacle in digital culture: Civic expression, fake news, and the role of media literacies in "post-fact" society'. *American Behavioral Scientist*, 61 (4), 441–54.

Mind (2021) *Body Dysmorphic Disorder (BDD)*. Accessed 27 November 2021. https://www.mind.org.uk/information-support/types-of-mental-health-problems/body-dysmorphic-disorder-bdd/about-bdd/.

Mok, W. S. Y. and Chan, W. W. L. (2016) 'How do tests and summary writing tasks enhance long-term retention of students with different levels of test anxiety?'. *Instructional Science*, 44 (6), 567–81. doi:10.1007/s11251-016-9393-x.

Molden, D. C. (2014) 'Understanding priming effects in social psychology: What is "social priming" and how does it occur?'. *Social Cognition*, 32, 1–11.

Molesworth, M., Nixon, E. and Scullion, R. (eds) (2011) *The Marketisation of Higher Education and the Student as Consumer*. London: Routledge.

Moore, A. (2014) *Understanding the School Curriculum: Theory, politics and principles*. London: Taylor and Francis.

Muckle, B. (2017) 'Equipping archaeology for the post-truth, fake news era'. *Anthropology News*, 58 (1), e164–7.

Murphy, R. (2013) 'Media roles in influencing the public understanding of educational assessment issues'. *Oxford Review of Education*, 39 (1), 139–50. doi:10.1080/03054985.2013.764760.

National Council on Measurement (1961) *The ... Yearbook of the National Council on Measurement in Education*. Ames: National Council on Measurement in Education.

Nebesnuick, D. (1990) *Monitoring & Evaluation and the 1988 Education Reform Act*. Slough: Education Management Information Exchange.

Newman, N. (2021) *Journalism, Media, and Technology Trends and Predictions 2021*. Oxford: Reuters Institute for the Study of Journalism. Accessed 27 November 2021. https://reutersinstitute. politics.ox.ac.uk/journalism-media-and-technology-trends-and-predictions-2021.

Newman, N., Fletcher, R., Schulz, A., Simge, A. and Kleis Nielsen, R. (2020) 'Reuters Institute Digital News Report 2020'. Accessed 9 January 2022. https://www.digitalnewsreport.org/ survey/2020/.

Newton, P. E. and Shaw, S. D. (2014) *Validity in Educational & Psychological Assessment*. London: SAGE Publications.

Ng, W. (2012) 'Can we teach digital natives digital literacy?'. *Computers and Education*, 59 (3), 1065–78. doi:10.1016/j.compedu.2012.04.016.

NHS Berkshire West (2020) *The Little Blue Book of Sunshine (Berkshire Edition)* (2nd edn). Reading: NHS Berkshire West. Accessed 25 March 2022. https://www.berkshirewestccg.nhs. uk/media/5349/lbbos-berkshire-edition-final.pdf.

Nisbet, I. and Shaw, S. D. (2019) 'Fair assessment viewed through the lenses of measurement theory'. *Assessment in Education: Principles, policy & practice*, 26 (5), 612–29. doi:10.1080/ 0969594X.2019.1586643.

Nisbet, I. and Shaw, S. D. (2020) *Is Assessment Fair?* London: SAGE Publications.

Nishiaki, Y. and Jöris, O. (2019) 'Learning among Neanderthals and Palaeolithic modern humans: Archaeological evidence', in Y. Nishiaki and O. Jöris (eds), *International Conference on Replacement of Neanderthals by Modern Humans*. Hokkaido: Springer Japan.

Norton, L., Floyd, S. and Norton, B. (2019) 'Lecturers' views of assessment design, marking and feedback in higher education: A case for professionalisation?'. *Assessment and Evaluation in Higher Education*, 44 (8), 1209–21. doi:10.1080/02602938.2019.1592110.

NSW Education Standards Authority (2020) *2019–20 Annual Report*. Accessed 19 January 2022. https://educationstandards.nsw.edu.au/wps/wcm/connect/2ca0e563-d566-47ce-8d29-a4529 7020b59/nesa-annual-report+2019-20.pdf?MOD=AJPERES&CVID=.

Nugent, R., Shannong, R., McNamee, H. and Molyneaux, F. (2015) *ICT & Me*. London: National Children's Bureau.

Nuttall, D. L. (1986) *Assessing Educational Achievement*. Brighton: Falmer Press.

Odejide, A. (1987) 'Education as quest: The Nigerian school story'. *Children's Literature in Education*, 18 (2), 77–87.

OECD (Organisation for Economic Co-operation and Development) (2005) *Formative Assessment Improving Learning in Secondary Classrooms*. Paris: OECD.

OECD (2008) 'New millennium learners: Initial findings on the effects of digital technolo- gies on school-age learners'. *OECD/CERI International Conference 'Learning in the 21st Century: Research, Innovation and Policy*. Accessed 27 November 2021. http://www.oecd.org/ site/educeri21st/40554230.pdf.

OECD (2010) *The Assessment of Higher Education Learning Outcomes*, *OECD Higher Education Programme Reports*. Accessed 27 November 2021. https://www.oecd.org/education/imhe/ theassessmentofhighereducationlearningoutcomes.htm.

OECD (2012) *Educational Research and Innovation Technology and Today's Learners*. Paris: OECD.

OECD (2015) *PISA 2015 Results, Vol. III: Students' Well-Being*. Paris: OECD.

OECD (2017) *Most Teenagers Happy with Their Lives but Schoolwork Anxiety and Bullying an Issue*. OECD Education Blog. Accessed 27 November 2021. https://www.oecd.org/education/most- teenagers-happy-with-their-lives-but-schoolwork-anxiety-and-bullying-an-issue.htm.

OECD (2018) *The Future of Education and Skills: Education 2030*. OECD Education Working Paper. Accessed 27 November 2021. http://www.oecd.org/education/2030/E2030 Position Paper (05.04.2018).pdf.

OECD (2019) *PISA 2018 Results, Vol. III: What School Life Means for Students*. Paris: OECD.

OECD (2020a) *Education at a Glance 2020 OECD Indicators*. Paris: OECD.

OECD (2020b) *PISA Test*. Accessed 27 November 2021. https://www.oecd.org/pisa/test/.

Office for Students (2020) *Analysis of Degree Classifications over Time*. Accessed 19 January 2022. https://www.officeforstudents.org.uk/publications/analysis-of-degree-classifications-over-time-changes-in-graduate-attainment-from-2010-11-to-2018-19/.

Ofqual (Office of Qualifications and Examinations Regulation) (2019) *Appeals for GCSE, AS and A level: Summer 2018 exam series*. Accessed 19 January 2022. https://www.gov.uk/government/statistics/appeals-for-gcse-as-and-a-level-summer-2018-exam-series.

Ogier, S. (ed.) (2019) *A Broad and Balanced Curriculum in Primary Schools: Educating the whole child*. London: SAGE Publication.

O'Hara, K. (2004) *Trust: From Socrates to spin*. London: Faber and Faber.

Okolie, U. C., Igwe, P. A., Nwosu, H. E., Eneje, B. C. and Mlanga, S. (2019) 'Enhancing graduate employability: Why do higher education institutions have problems with teaching generic skills?'. *Policy Futures in Education*, 18 (2), 294–313. doi:10.1177/1478210319864824.

O'Neill, O. (2013) 'Intelligent accountability in education'. *Oxford Review of Education*, 39 (1), 4–16.

Open Textbook Library (2016) *Communication in the Real World*. University of Minnesota Libraries Publishing.

Orbach, S. (2010) *Bodies*. London: Profile.

Osborne, M. (2010) 'Policy and practice in widening participation: A six country comparative study of access as flexibility'. *International Journal of Lifelong Education*, 22 (1), 43–58. doi:10.1080/02601370304826.

Oxford English Dictionary (n.d.) 'snowflake, n.' Accessed 27 November 2021. https://www.oed.com/view/Entry/183512?redirectedFrom=snowflake&amp.

Palfrey, J. and Gasser, U. (eds) (2008) *Born Digital: Understanding the first generation of digital natives*. New York: Basic Books.

Papamichail, M. and Sharma, N. (2019) *Left to Their Own Devices: Young people, social media and mental health*. London: Barnardo's. Accessed 9 January 2022. https://www.barnardos.org.uk/sites/default/files/uploads/Executive%20Summary.pdf.

Pearson UK (2021) *Policy Watch*. Accessed 27 November 2021. https://www.pearson.com/uk/news-and-policy/policy-watch.html.

Pellegrino, J. W. and Hilton, M. L. (2012) *Education for Life and Work*. Washington, DC: National Academies Press. doi:10.17226/13398.

Perryman, J., Ball, S., Maguire, M. and Braun, A. (2011). 'Life in the pressure cooker: School league tables and English and Mathematics teachers' responses to accountability in a results-driven era'. *British Journal of Educational Studies*, 59 (2), 179–95. doi:10.1080/00071005.2011.578568.

Pesold, U. (2017) *The Other in the School Stories*. Leiden and Boston: Brill Rodopi. doi:10.1163/9789004341722.

Peters, R. S. (2015) *Ethics and Education (Routledge Revivals)*. London: Routledge. doi:10.4324/9781315712383.

Phillips, K. A. (1996) *The Broken Mirror: Understanding and treating body dysmorphic disorder*. Oxford: Oxford University Press.

Piaget, J. (2014) 'Advances in child and adolescent psychology', in P. Light, S. Sheldon and M. Woodhead (eds), *Learning to Think*. London: Taylor and Francis, 5–15.

Pink, S. (2007) *Doing Visual Ethnography: Images, media and representation in research* (2nd edn). London: SAGE Publications.

Pinker, S. (2018) 'The media exaggerates negative news. This distortion has consequences', *The Guardian*, 17 February. Accessed 27 November 2021. https://www.theguardian.com/commentisfree/2018/feb/17/steven-pinker-media-negative-news.

Pope, W. J. (1888) 'Payment by results: Presidential address', in National Union of Elementary Teachers (ed.), *Nineteenth Conference of the National Union of Elementary Teachers*. London: Alexander and Shephard.

Popham, W. J. (2017) *The ABCs of Educational Testing*. London: SAGE Publications.

Postman, N. (2011) *The End of Education: Redefining the value of school*. New York: Vintage.

Potter, J. and Wetherell, M. (1994) 'Analyzing discourse', in A. Bryman and B. Burgess (eds), *Analyzing Qualitative Data*. London: Routledge.

Poydar, N. (2005) *The Biggest Test in the Universe*. New York: Holiday House.

Prażmo, E. M. (2019) '"Leftie snowflakes" and other metaphtonymies in the British political discourse'. *Journal of Language and Politics*, 18 (3), 371–92. doi:10.1075/jlp.17073.pra.

Prensky, M. (2001) *Digital Natives, Digital Immigrants*. Bingley: MCB University Press.

Putwain, D. W. (2008) 'Deconstructing test anxiety'. *Emotional and Behavioural Difficulties*, 13 (2), 141–55. doi:10.1080/13632750802027713.

Putwain, D. W. and Daly, A. L. (2014) 'Test anxiety prevalence and gender differences in a sample of English secondary school students'. *Educational Studies*, 40 (5), 554–70. doi:10.1080/03055698.2014.953914.

Putwain, D. W., Daly, A. L., Chamberlain, S. and Sadreddini, S. (2016) '"Sink or swim": Buoyancy and coping in the cognitive test anxiety–academic performance relationship'. *Educational Psychology*, 36 (10), 1807–25. doi:10.1080/01443410.2015.1066493.

Putwain, D. W. and von der Embse, N. P. (2018) 'Teachers use of fear appeals and timing reminders prior to high-stakes examinations: Pressure from above, below, and within'. *Social Psychology of Education*, 21 (5), 1001–19. doi:10.1007/s11218-018-9448-8.

Ragusa, A. T. and Bousfield, K. (2015) '"It's not the test, it's how it's used!" Critical analysis of public response to NAPLAN and MySchool Senate Inquiry'. *British Journal of Sociology of Education*, 38 (3), 265–86. doi:10.1080/01425692.2015.1073100.

Reay, D. and Wiliam, D. (1999) '"I'll be a nothing": Structure, agency and the construction of identity through assessment'. *British Educational Research Journal*, 25 (3), 343–54. doi:10.1080/0141192990250305.

Reiss, M. J. and White, J. (2013) *An Aims-Based Curriculum: The significance of human flourishing for schools* (Bedford Way Papers 39). London: IOE Press.

Richardson, M. and Clesham, R. (2021) 'Rise of the machines? The evolving role of AI technologies in high-stakes assessment'. *London Review of Education*, 19 (1), 9. doi:10.14324/LRE.19.1.09.

Richardson, M. and Healy, M. (2019) 'Examining the ethical environment in higher education'. *British Educational Research Journal*, 1089–104. doi:10.1002/berj.3552.

Richardson, M., Hernández-Hernández, F., Hiltunen, M., Moura, A., Fulková, M., King, F. and Collins, F. M. (2020) 'Creative connections: The power of contemporary art to explore European citizenship'. *London Review of Education*, 18 (2), 10. doi:10.14324/LRE.18.2.10.

Richardson, M., Isaacs, T., Barnes, I., Swensson, C., Wilkinson, D. and Golding, J. (2020) *Trends in International Mathematics and Science Study (TIMSS) 2019: National report for England: Research report: December 2020*. London: Department for Education.

Roberts, J. A. and David, M. E. (2019) 'The social media party: Fear of missing out (FoMO), social media intensity, connection, and well-being'. *International Journal of Human–Computer Interaction*, 36 (4), 386–92. doi:10.1080/10447318.2019.1646517.

Roberts-Holmes, G. and Bradbury, A. (2016a) 'Governance, accountability and the datafication of early years education in England'. *British Educational Research Journal*, 42 (4), 600–13. doi:10.1002/berj.3221.

Roberts-Holmes, G. and Bradbury, A. (2016b) 'The datafication of early years education and its impact upon pedagogy'. *Improving Schools*, 19 (2), 119–28.

Robertson, S. L. (2005) 'Re-imagining and rescripting the future of education: Global knowledge economy discourses and the challenge to education systems'. *Comparative Education*, 41 (2), 151–70.

Rorty, R. (1980) *Philosophy and the Mirror of Nature*. Oxford: Blackwell.

Rowling, J. K. (1997) *Harry Potter and the Philosopher's Stone*. London: Bloomsbury.

Rowling, J. K. (1998) *Harry Potter and the Chamber of Secrets*. London: Bloomsbury.

Rowling, J. K. (1999) *Harry Potter and the Prisoner of Azkaban*. London: Bloomsbury.

Rowling, J. K. (2000) *Harry Potter and the Goblet of Fire*. London: Bloomsbury.

Rowling, J. K. (2004) *Harry Potter and the Order of the Phoenix*. London: Bloomsbury.

Rowling, J. K. (2006) *Harry Potter and the Half-Blood Prince*. London: Bloomsbury.

Rowling, J. K. (2007) *Harry Potter and the Deathly Hallows*. London: Bloomsbury.

Rust, C. (2007) 'Towards a scholarship of assessment'. *Assessment & Evaluation in Higher Education*, 32 (2): 229–37. doi:10.1080/02602930600805192.

Safi, M. (2018) 'India's "cheating mafia" gets to work as school exam season hits', *The Guardian*, 3 April. Accessed 27 November 2021. https://www.theguardian.com/world/2018/apr/03/india-school-exam-season-cheating-mafia-#:~:text=A%20few%20minutes%20into%20the,he%20was%20sent%20days%20before.

Sandel, M. J. (2007) *The Case Against Perfection*. Cambridge, MA: Harvard University Press.

Sapienza, Z. S., Iyer, N. and Veenstra, A. S. (2015) 'Reading Lasswell's model of communication backward: Three scholarly misconceptions'. *Mass Communication and Society*, 18 (5), 599–622. doi:10.1080/15205436.2015.1063666.

Sarason, S. B. (ed.) (1960) *Anxiety in Elementary School Children: A report of research*. New York: Wiley.

Sarason, S. B. (1964) 'A longitudinal study of the relation of test anxiety to performance on intelligence and achievement tests'. *Monographs of the Society for Research in Child Development*, 29 (7), 1–51.

Saunders, L. (1995) *Education for Life: The cross-curricular themes in primary and secondary schools*. Slough: National Foundation for Educational Research.

Schmidtz, D. and Brighouse, H. (2020) *Debating Education: Is there a role for markets?* Oxford: Oxford University Press.

The School Reading List (2021) 'Magazines for children and teenagers: Our top picks'. Accessed 27 November 2021. https://schoolreadinglist.co.uk/resources/magazines-and-newspapers-for-children-and-teenagers/.

Scollon, R. (2008) *Analyzing Public Discourse*. London: Riverhead Books.

Scott, D. (2017) *Education Systems and Learners*. London: Palgrave Macmillan.

SEAB (Singapore Examinations and Assessment Board) (n.d.) *Academic Publications*. Accessed 19 January 2022. https://www.seab.gov.sg/home/services/academic-publications.

Segool, N. K., Carlson, J. S., Goforth, A. N., Von der Embse, N. and Barterian, J. A. (2013) 'Heightened test anxiety among young children: Elementary school students' anxious responses to high-stakes testing'. *Psychology in the Schools*, 50 (5), 489–99. doi:10.1002/pits.21689.

Shute, V. J. (2008) 'Focus on formative feedback'. *Review of Educational Research*, 78 (1), 153–89. doi:10.3102/0034654307313795.

Simpson, D. J., Jackson, J. C. and Aycock, J. C. (eds) (2005) *John Dewey and the Art of Teaching Toward Reflective and Imaginative Practice*. Thousand Oaks: SAGE Publications.

Singer, J. B. (2010) 'Journalism ethics amid structural change'. *Daedalus*, 139 (2), 89–99. doi:10.1162/daed.2010.139.2.89.

Smith, A. N. (2018) 'Pursuing "Generation Snowflake": Mr. Robot and the USA Network's Mission for Millennials'. *Television & New Media*, 20 (5), 443–59. doi:10.1177/1527476418789896.

Smith, E. and Gorard, S. (2005) '"They don't give us our marks": The role of formative feedback in student progress'. *Assessment in Education: Principles, policy & practice*, 12 (1), 21–38. doi:10.1080/0969594042000333896.

Snyder, B. R. (1973) *The Hidden Curriculum*. Cambridge, MA: MIT Press.

Sorrell, T. (1990) 'The world from its own point of view', in A. R. Malachowski (ed.), *Reading Rorty*. Oxford: Blackwell.

Spielman, A. and Ofsted (2018) *HMCI Commentary: Curriculum and the new education inspection framework*. Accessed 21 November 2021. https://www.gov.uk/government/speeches/hmci-commentary-curriculum-and-the-new-education-inspection-framework.

Standards and Testing Agency (2021) *Maladministration Reports*. Accessed 19 January 2022. https://www.gov.uk/government/collections/maladministration-reports.

Statista (2020) *UK Student Loan Debt 2020, Statista, Education and Science Statistical Summaries*. Accessed 27 November 2021. https://www.statista.com/statistics/376423/uk-student-loan-debt/.

Stenhouse, L. (1975) *An Introduction to Curriculum Research and Development*. London: Heinemann Educational.

Stiggins, R. (1991) 'Assessment literacy'. *Phi Delta Kappan*, 72 (7), 534–9.

Stiggins, R. (1993) 'Two disciplines of educational assessment'. *Measurement and Evaluation in Counseling and Development*, 26 (1), 93–104.

Stiggins, R. (1995) 'Assessment literacy for the 21st century'. *Phi Delta Kappan*, 77 (3), 238–45.

Stiggins, R. (2014) 'Improve assessment literacy outside of schools too'. *Phi Delta Kappan*, 96 (2), 67–72.

Stobart, G. (2008) *Testing Times: The uses and abuses of assessment*. London: Routledge. doi:10.4324/9780203930502.

Stobart, G. (2014) *The Expert Learner Challenging the Myth of Ability*. Maidenhead: McGraw-Hill Education.

Stromquist, N. P. (2002) *Education in a Globalized World: The connectivity of economic power, technology, and knowledge*. Lanham, MD: Rowman & Littlefield.

Sud, A. (2001) 'Test anxiety research in India: Twentieth century in retrospect'. *Psychology and Developing Societies*, 13 (1), 51–69. doi:10.1177/097133360101300103.

Suissa, J. (2008) 'Happiness lessons in schools'. *Journal of Philosophy of Education*, 42 (3–4), 575–90.

Suiter, J. (2016) 'Post-truth politics'. *Political Insight*, 7 (3), 25–7.

Sutch, T. and Klir, N. (2017) *Tweeting about Exams: Investigating the use of social media over the summer 2016 session*. Accessed 11 January 2022. https://www.cambridgeassessment.org.uk/Images/375441-tweeting-about-exams-investigating-the-use-of-social-media-over-the-summer-2016-session.pdf.

Tan, C. (2013) *Learning from Shanghai: Lessons on achieving educational success*. Dordrecht: Springer. doi:10.1007/978-981-4021-87-6_10.

Taylor, K. R. (2003) 'When students sue teachers over grades'. *The Education Digest*, 68 (6), 58–63.

Thompson, G. (2010) 'Local experiences, global similarities: Teacher perceptions of the impacts of national testing', in B. Lingard, G. Thompson and S. Sellar (eds), *National Testing in Schools: An Australian assessment*. Abingdon: Routledge.

Tomlinson, M. (2008) '"The degree is not enough": Students' perceptions of the role of higher education credentials for graduate work and employability'. *British Journal of Sociology of Education*. doi:10.1080/01425690701737457.

Torrance, H. (2017) 'Blaming the victim: Assessment, examinations, and the responsibilisation of students and teachers in neo-liberal governance'. *Discourse: Studies in the Cultural Politics of Education*, 38 (1), 83–96. doi:10.1080/01596306.2015.1104854.

Trowler, P. (2003) *Change Thinking, Change Practices: A guide to change for heads of department, programme leaders and other change agents in higher education*. York: Learning and Teaching Support Network.

Tunc-Aksan, A. and Akbay, S. E. (2019) 'Smartphone addiction, fear of missing out, and perceived competence as predictors of social media addiction of adolescents'. *European Journal of Educational Research*, 8 (2). doi:10.12973/eu-jer.8.2.559.

UCL (2021) 'UCL makes formal public apology for its history and legacy of eugenics'. *UCL News*, 7 January. Accessed 27 November 2021. https://www.ucl.ac.uk/news/2021/jan/ucl-makes-formal-public-apology-its-history-and-legacy-eugenics.

UNESCO (United Nations Educational, Scientific and Cultural Organization) (2020) *Education in a Post-COVID World: Nine ideas for public action International Commission on the Futures of Education*. Paris: UNESCO.

Universities and Colleges Admissions Service (2018) *Qualification Information Profile: China, Online*. Accessed 25 March 2022. https://qips.ucas.com/qip/china-gaokao.

Universities UK International (2019) *International Graduate Outcomes 2019*. London: Universities UK. Accessed 27 November 2021. https://www.universitiesuk.ac.uk/International/Documents/international_graduate_outcomes.pdf.

Unterhalter, E. (2019) *Measuring the Unmeasurable in Education*. London: Routledge.

Van Der Kleij, F. M., Cumming, J. J. and Looney, A. (2018) 'Policy expectations and support for teacher formative assessment in Australian education reform'. *Assessment in Education: Principles, policy & practice*, 25 (6), 620–37. doi:10.1080/0969594X.2017.1374924.

van Dijck, J. (2013) *The Culture of Connectivity*. Oxford: Oxford University Press.

Van Hout, T. and Van Leuven, S. (2016) 'Investigating "churnalism" in real-time news', in B. Franklin and S. A. Elridge (eds), *The Routledge Companion to Digital Journalism Studies*. London: Routledge, Chapter 11.

Volante, L. and Fazio, X. (2007) 'Exploring teacher candidates' assessment literacy: Implications for teacher education reform and professional development'. *Canadian Journal of Education*, 30 (3), 749–70. doi:10.2307/20466661.

Von der Embse, N., Barterian, J. and Segool, N. (2013) 'Test anxiety interventions for children and adolescents: A systematic review of treatment studies from 2000–2010'. *Psychology in the Schools*, 50 (1), 57–71. doi:10.1002/pits.21660.

von der Embse, N. and Hasson, R. (2012) 'Test anxiety and high-stakes test performance between school settings: Implications for Educators'. *Preventing School Failure: Alternative education for children and youth*, 56 (3), 180–7. doi:10.1080/1045988X.2011.633285.

Walker, A. and Qian, H. (2018) 'Exploring the mysteries of school success in Shanghai'. *ECNU Review of Education*, 1 (1), 119–34. doi:10.30926/ecnuroe2018010107.

Wang, P., Angarita, R. and Renna, I. (2018) 'Is this the era of misinformation yet: Combining social bots and fake news to deceive the masses'. *WWW'18: Companion Proceedings of the World Wide Web Conference, 2018*, 1557–61. doi:10.1145/3184558.3191610.

Warmington, P. and Murphy, R. (2004) 'Could do better? Media depictions of UK educational assessment results'. *Journal of Education Policy* 19 (3), 285–99. doi:10.1080/0268093042000207629.

Warmington, P. and Murphy, R. (2007) '"Read all about it!" UK news media coverage of A-Level results'. *Policy Futures in Education*, 5 (1), 70–83. doi:10.2304/pfie.2007.5.1.70.

We Are Social UK and Hootsuite (2021) *Digital 2021 April Global Statshot*. Accessed 27 November 2021. https://wearesocial.com/uk/blog/2021/04/60-percent-of-the-worlds-population-is-now-online.

White, J. (2009) *The Aims of Education Restated*. London: Psychology Press.

White, J. (2014). *Who Needs Examinations: A story of climbing ladders and dodging snakes.* London: IOE Press.

Wigfield, A. and Eccles, J. S. (1990) 'Test anxiety in the school setting', in M. Lewis and S. M. Miller (eds), *Handbook of Developmental Psychopathology.* Boston: Springer, 237–50. doi:10.1007/978-1-4615-7142-1_19.

Wiliam, D. (1993) 'Reconceptualising validity, dependability and reliability for National Curriculum assessment'. Paper given at the British Educational Research Association (BERA) conference. Liverpool University.

Wiliam, D. (2001) *Level Best? Levels of attainment in national curriculum assessment.* Accessed 29 November 2021. https://www.dylanwiliam.org/Dylan_Wiliams_website/Papers_files/Level%20best%20-%20Levels%20of%20attainment%20in%20the%20national%20curriculum%20%28ATL%202001%29.pdf.

Wiliam, D. (2009) *Assessment for Learning: Why, what and how?* London: IOE Press.

Wiliam, D. (2016) *Leadership for Teacher Learning: Creating a culture where all teachers improve so that all students succeed.* Florida: Learning Sciences International.

Wiliam, D. (2017) 'Assessment and learning: some reflections'. *Assessment in Education: Principles, policy and practice*, 24 (3), 394–403. doi:10.1080/0969594X.2017.1318108.

Woodward-Smith, E. (2011) 'Sociocultural references in context: The school story subculture'. *Working Papers on English Studies*, 18, 243–64.

World Economic Forum (2018) *Global Competitiveness Index: 2018*. Accessed 27 November 2021. https://reports.weforum.org/global-competitiveness-index-2017-2018/competitiveness-rankings/#series=GCI.A.04.02.

Wyatt-Smith, C. and Cumming, J. (2009) *Educational Assessment in the 21st Century: Connecting theory and practice.* Dordrecht: Springer.

Xie, X. (2002) *Quality Education in China EQO (Essential-qualities-oriented) Education.* Accessed 27 November 2021. http://epedagog.upol.cz/eped1.2002/mimo/clanek02.htm.

YouGov (2019a) *Perceptions of A Levels, GCSEs and Other Qualifications in England – Wave 17.* Accessed 19 January 2022. https://www.gov.uk/government/statistics/perceptions-of-a-levels-gcses-and-other-qualifications-wave-17.

YouGov (2019b) *Perceptions of AS/A levels, GCSEs and Applied General qualifications in England-Wave 17.* Accessed 10 January 2022. https://assets.publishing.service.gov.uk/government/uploads/system/uploads/attachment_data/file/792298/Perceptions_Survey_Wave_17_-_Background_Information.pdf.

YouGov (2020) *Perceptions of AS/A levels, GCSEs and Applied General qualifications in England – Wave 18.* Accessed 27 November 2021. https://assets.publishing.service.gov.uk/government/uploads/system/uploads/attachment_data/file/896440/Perceptions_Survey_Wave_18_-_Report.pdf.

YoungMinds (2017) *Exam Stress*. Accessed 27 November 2021. https://youngminds.org.uk/find-help/feelings-and-symptoms/exam-stress/.

Zappavigna, M. (2013) *Discourse of Twitter and Social Media: How we use language to create affiliation on the web.* London: Bloomsbury.

Zarrin, S. A., Gracia, E. and Paixão, M. P. (2020) 'Prediction of academic procrastination by fear of failure and self-regulation'. *Educational Sciences: Theory and Practice*, 20 (3), 34–43. doi:10.12738/jestp.2020.3.003.

Zeidner, M. (2007) 'Test anxiety in educational contexts. Concepts, findings, and future directions', in P. A. Schutz and R. Pekrun (eds) *Emotion in Education*. London: Academix Press, 165–84. doi:10.1016/B978-012372545-5/50011-3.

Zhang, S., Woodman, T. and Roberts, R. (2018) 'Anxiety and fear in sport and performance', *Oxford Research Encyclopedia of Psychology*. doi:10.1093/acrefore/9780190236557.013.162.

Zimdars, M. and McLeod, K. (eds) (2020) *Fake News: Understanding media and misinformation in the digital age.* Cambridge, MA: MIT Press.

Index

Lightning Source UK Ltd.
Milton Keynes UK
UKHW021935190722
406090UK00003B/147